McCall's
Do-It-Yourself Traditional Decorating
By Phyllis Hingston Roderick

RANDOM HOUSE/THE McCALL PATTERN COMPANY/NEW YORK, NEW YORK

All rights reserved under International and Pan-American Copyright
Conventions. Published in the United States by Random House, Inc.,
New York, and simultaneously in Canada by Random House of Canada
Limited, Toronto. Library of Congress Cataloging in Publication Data:
Roderick, Phyllis Hingston. McCall's do-it-yourself traditional decorat-
ing. 1. Drapery. 2. Coverlets. 3. Interior decoration—Amateurs' manuals.
I. Title.   II. Title: Do-it-yourself traditional decorating.   TT387.R63
747'.8'8   74-6096   ISBN 0-394-49065-7   Manufactured in the United
States of America   First Edition

300 Years of American History

Interior design is more than a decorative art. It's an accurate indication of the economic, political and social climate of any era. Because it undertakes to define and describe America's most prevalent decorating styles and the forces that made them fashionable or expedient as they developed and changed over a period of three hundred years, this book is, to some extent, a history book. But it brings that history up to date by showing you how to capture the mood, the look and the spirit of America's traditional decorating styles and adapt them for today's homes. It also shows you how, via detailed diagrams and directions, to duplicate some of the characteristic furnishings and accessories—the all-important draperies, valances and cornices, the bedspreads, bolsters and bed-canopies—that help give period rooms their distinctive flavor.

CONTENTS

Turn-of-the-Century Nostalgia

Defining a period when interior "design" did not exist, and the desire for decorative reform inspired the phenomenon known as "Art Nouveau." How to translate the heterogeneous scramble of styles that prevailed at the turn of the century into room settings of eclectic charm with a welcome touch of whimsy.

The Past-and-Present Look

Tradition brought up to date for today's homes. The popular decorating style that blends comfortable traditional furniture into a contemporary setting; many attractive ways to achieve this kind of eclectic ambiance, including mixing Oriental pieces with contemporary furniture and 20th-Century fabrics.

Window Treatments for Traditional Rooms

How to make swagged draperies in the 18th-Century manner; traditional shirred-top draperies that form a self-valance; a scalloped cornice and draperies with a touch of Chinoiserie; print-lined draperies to complement any color scheme, including an easy formula for determining width of pinch pleats.

The Well-Dressed Bed

Bed treatments inspired by Colonial four-posters and English Regency tent-beds and how to make them, from a head-of-the-bed valance and draperies that scale the four-poster look down to small-room size, to a full-fledged four-poster treatment with dramatic scalloped canopy and contrast-lined drapery.

The Early American Look

authentic in every detail

Very few period styles can be picked up and used intact without seeming out of place in the context of today. Early American is one of those few. The simple, sturdy furniture, so forthright and so functional, has a timeless integrity that transcends fads and fashions. And the honest, unaffected look of the early American style suits many contemporaries who crave a natural, down-to-earth environment.

If you admire true 17th-Century Americana, the room at the right is your kind of thing. Although it looks every inch authentic, it's done with present-day adaptations, even the furniture that looks handhewn. You can find excellent reproductions of typical pieces, such as the monk's bench that tilts down to become a table. The crewel-patterned fabric is printed cotton, but like many that can be found today, the design closely copies the painstakingly embroidered original.

When, where and how it all began

"Early American" is the overworked label that has been indiscriminately applied to everything that happened in American interior design from the 17th through the 19th Century. To many people it is synonymous with spinning wheels, rag rugs and the ubiquitous cobbler's-bench-turned-planter. To others, it evokes Adam fireplaces, Chippendale side chairs and painted woodwork. But Early American is more than either of these. It is, to be precise, a series of interpretations of European styles spanning roughly two hundred years and adapted from five different countries. While the more refined styles of colonial America in the 18th Century, and even the nationalistic motifs of the Federal era are often lumped together with 17th Century styles under the grab-bag title of Early American, we will consider here only the earliest Early American period—the "Pilgrim Century" that included the years from 1608 to 1720.

What was happening

These were the years when the earliest settlers dared the uncertainties of a whole New World. Inspired by political and religious oppression, most of the emigrants ventured from England. Smaller groups arrived from Holland and Germany—the former to settle in the wilds of New York, the latter to colonize southeastern Pennsylvania. These intrepid souls brought with them customs, tastes, and—as best they could—tools for building a brave new world. Plymouth (Massachusetts) in the north, and Jamestown (Virginia) in the south became the centers of the loosely-grouped settlements.

Most of those who settled in the north were religious enthusiasts, the Pilgrims and the Puritans. Their towns grew up around their churches. Their farms were small and agricultural enterprise limited because it was difficult to clear the land of boulders. Thus the northern settlers turned to the small industries of fur trading, fishing and shipbuilding.

In the south, by contrast, the land was fertile, and a wealthier, agrarian economy soon began to flourish. Farms grew into plantations, and the owners started to live like lords in elaborate dwellings, surrounded by imported luxuries little known in the north. But north *or* south, the earliest settlers shared the same basic struggle . . . the struggle for survival against weather, animals and Indians.

How 17th-Century homes were built

The first colonists undoubtedly lived in the crudest of huts until trees could be felled to supply the logs which at first were stood on end and covered with thatched roofs. The traditional log cabin, with logs laid horizontally, was brought to America by the Swedes a few years later. Due to the industry and ingenuity of the early settlers, these rudimentary dwellings were soon supplanted by the simple but substantial frame houses we now call Early American. Extensive pine forests had to be cleared before the land could be used, so lumber was abundant, and the homes were usually made entirely of wood. The structural beams and posts were left visible in their natural, rough-hewn state. Doors and the woodwork framing windows also went unpainted. The main beam, called the *summer beam,* ran through the center of the house and rested on the stone chimney.

Parlor from the Thomas Hart house built in Ipswich, Massachusetts, before 1675; now in The American Wing of The Metropolitan Museum of Art, New York City, New York

The most typical houses were divided into two rooms, with a double-faced stone fireplace in the center. One side faced each room, set in a wall of unfinished horizontal or vertical pine planking. As the wood aged it also mellowed, adding rich dark warmth to the rooms. The other interior walls were plastered with a mixture of clay and animal hair.

One of the two rooms was a combination kitchen, dining and living room. The other served as a bedroom for the whole family. As the family grew, wings were added to the ground floor and dormer windows to the roof so an attic room could also be added. Ceilings, by today's standards, were low, about seven feet from the floor.

Windows were of the casement type, with small rectangular, round, or diamond-shaped panes. The panes were made of glass, oiled paper or isinglass, separated by lead stripping. In some houses, wooden blinds were used instead of glass panes, and sometimes the two were combined.

The earliest floors were simply packed earth. These were succeeded by stone floors and finally by wide planks of pine, oak or chestnut. Occasionally, small Oriental rugs or heavy tapestries were scattered about the otherwise bare floors.

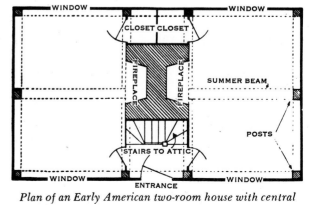

Plan of an Early American two-room house with central chimney

What Early American furniture was like

American furniture of the Pilgrim Century, like the prevailing architecture of the period, consisted primarily of provincial versions of English Jacobean and Restoration styles. Where the settlers were of Dutch, German or French origin, the influence of the homeland was also visible. But these variations were neither so numerous nor so significant as their English counterparts.

In any case, the homes were sparsely furnished, with rarely anything but the bare essentials included. The colonists could bring very little with them from Europe, so practically all furniture had to be made by the same craftsmen who built the houses. And since most of the pieces were reproduced from memory, the copies were necessarily crude.

Living room pieces were limited to chests, cupboards, turned or wainscot chairs, stools, settles, the desk box, a trestle table, perhaps a smaller table and space-saving furniture such as the table-chair and gate-leg tables. Bedroom furniture consisted of crude four-poster and trundle beds, wooden cradles, and a few chests for storage. Non-essentials such as clocks and mirrors were rare.

Fabrics were limited to a few imported silks and some needlework and embroidery worked on basic materials which also had to be imported. Patterns, therefore, were also limited, usually to stylized florals and variations on the flame stitch.

The pieces of furniture were box-like or rectangular in design, making no concessions to the roundness of the human body. Ornamentation, although crudely executed, was often extensive, and included strapwork carving, turned legs and bannisters, applied split spindles and some painted decoration. The carvings included low-relief copies of English motifs such as the Tudor rose, tulips, sunflowers, acanthus leaves and three-part arcaded panels.

Copying the original English pieces, oak and walnut were favored for furniture, but the more common native woods such as pine, beech, ash, cherry, maple and cedar were frequently used. Two different woods were often combined in the same piece of furniture.

The principal differences between 17th-Century American furniture and that of Jacobean England were in the color, the scale and the degree of refinement in decoration. American oak and walnut were lighter-grained than the English varieties, and although the rectangular construction of the original pieces was retained, American furniture was smaller in scale to suit the smaller rooms and low ceilings. The tools necessary for fine craftsmanship were limited in the colonies, so ornamentation was cruder.

The most important individual pieces

The most characteristic piece of furniture in the 17th-Century home was the chest. It was utilized for seating as well as for storage. The earliest chests stood flat on the floor or on squat supports. The tops were hinged for easy access, and some included a drawer at the bottom. Later, legs were added, the top fastened down for display of china and candles, and the entire storage area divided into drawers. Thus the simple chest became the popular chest of drawers.

In the meantime, two characteristic styles of chests developed—the *Connecticut chest* and the *Hadley chest,* both of which were manufactured in Connecticut. The Connecticut chest stood on short legs and had two rows of drawers below the

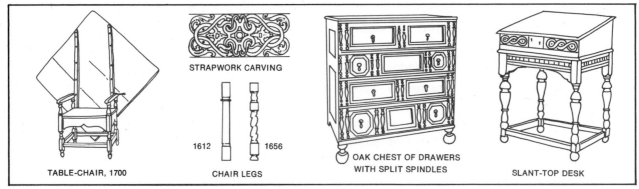

TABLE-CHAIR, 1700

STRAPWORK CARVING

1612   1656

CHAIR LEGS

OAK CHEST OF DRAWERS WITH SPLIT SPINDLES

SLANT-TOP DESK

storage area. It was made of oak and decorated with split spindles painted black to imitate ebony. The drawer pulls were ovals placed diagonally. The Hadley chest had only one drawer and was decorated with crude incised ornamentation. The face of the upper portion was divided into three indented panels carved with flower and leaf patterns. Chests placed on higher legs evolved into cupboards, retaining the split spindle and panelled decoration.

Another top-opening small chest had a slanted lid and carved oak sides. It was used as storage for books, writing materials and the family Bible. The *desk-box,* as it was called, was originally placed on top of a larger chest or a table. But eventually it, too, was placed on legs, evolving into the slant-top desk.

Most of the tables of the period had turned legs. Some were small and rectangular, with molded stretchers. Others were round, drop-leaf tables with a variety of supports for the leaf, such as swinging arms, butterfly wings or gate legs. The largest were of the trestle type, with pine tops and oak frames. They were frequently covered with tapestries or Oriental carpets.

Chairs were scarce and anything but luxurious. They were rectangular, firm, and devoid of upholstery. Occasionally, cushions were placed on the seats, but these did little to alter the austerity of the pieces. In each home there was an oak *wainscot chair* which served as the seat of honor. It had a carved panel back, curved arms and turned legs. The *Brewster chair* and its somewhat plainer relative, the *Carver chair,* had turned legs (those in the rear formed the back uprights), turned stretchers and both vertical and horizontal turned spindles. A similar type of chair, the *slat-back,* had ladder rails between the back stretchers. With the exception of the wainscot chair, these all had rush seats.

At the end of the century, the influence of the Restoration was felt when the William and Mary style was introduced. For one thing, there were noticeable changes in the way wooden chairs were made. Seats and backs acquired inserts of cane. The Flemish scroll ornament came into use, and S- and C-shaped curves were seen in backs and stretchers. Walnut began to replace the formerly-favored oak. Less cumbersome side chairs with spiral turned legs and padded seats and backs covered in "Turkey work" tapestry came into fashion.

The hardware and lighting fixtures of the 17th Century were of the simplest types, because utility was the primary consideration. Latches, bolts and hinges were made of wrought iron. Candlestands and candlesticks were of iron, tin or pewter. One characteristic means of lighting was the *Betty lamp.* Similar to Egyptian and Roman lamps, it hung from the mantel of the fireplace. And old wagon wheels were often utilized for chandeliers by attaching brackets to hold candles.

In the year 1700 Herculaneum was discovered; Pompeii came to light a few years later. The excitement and excavations that resulted inspired the great classical revival of the 18th Century. Its effect on the arts, on architecture and on all forms of decoration changed the face of Europe, but came slowly to the colonies. The homes of Pennsylvania and Virginia were the first to show evidence of the sweeping new classicism, and as time went on, other settlements along the coast felt the impact of the European movement. But the colonists pushing westward carried the 17th Century styles with them right into the 1800's.

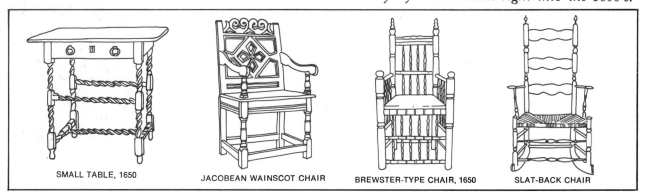

SMALL TABLE, 1650   JACOBEAN WAINSCOT CHAIR   BREWSTER-TYPE CHAIR, 1650   SLAT-BACK CHAIR

$\mathcal{E}$arly $\mathcal{A}$merican
is a mixture; interpret it to suit your taste

The term "Early American" as it is most commonly used refers to a longer time-span than the "Pilgrim Century" alone. It encompasses the evolution of furniture and living styles that continued from the days of the earliest settlers through the Revolutionary War. That is what makes the term so inclusive and the concept so easy to work with. There are more variations within the style than in any other period style of decorating, and the various regional styles and pieces from different periods within the total time-span blend together beautifully. For one thing, the many styles within the style all share a feeling of livability and warmth. And most can be successfully mixed together to suit your particular taste. Indeed, successful Early American rooms are almost always a mixture of styles, with a harmonious over-all effect. The originators of the style, those rugged individualists devoted to enterprise and function, would be the first to encourage you to adapt their ideas to your 20th-Century way of life. So having first shown a practically letter-perfect 17th-Century room for Early American purists, here follow a few to which have been added companionable pieces from neighboring eras, as well as some contemporary elements, to give each room an unstudied, livable look, which is, after all, the essence of the Early American style.

In the earliest years of "Early America," activity in the home centered around the huge, walk-in fireplace. The ceilings were low, beams exposed, walls left unpainted. Updating this rustic look, the sides of the brick fireplace here have been extended and framed with beams, and the picture window has been given a simple, contemporary treatment. Two wing-back chairs from the later Seaport Colonial style add a touch of elegance. Directions for slipcovering wing chairs of any style begin on Page 26.

ERNEST SILVA

Early American
in spirit

The idea is the thing. The look, the spirit, the ambiance that prevailed when our nation was young is what appeals to so many people today. It's not necessary to create a museum-like room to capture the charm of the Early American period. It's the functional simplicity, the warmth and flavor of the style you want. So if you like the cozy look of a curtained and canopied four-poster bed, have it–even without the four-poster! And if you love the austerity of Early American furniture, but your family like a contemporary approach to pattern and color, have both. It's *your* room.

The "four-poster" bed above is an engaging fake, easy to construct with the directions that follow. (There aren't any posters at all.) The clean, spare look of the room is typically Early American, but is also closely related to contemporary.

American Provincial, also known as New England Colonial, is perhaps the most familiar Early American style. Its rustic charm is exemplified by sturdy country furniture such as the hutch cabinet, trestle table and ladderback chairs seen here. The metal chandelier sheds more light on the way things were back then. But the fabric-covered wall above the painted chair rail and wainscoting brings the room forward in time, adding the bold pattern and color so favored today.

$\mathcal{E}$arly $\mathcal{A}$merican
in color

The color schemes of the "Pilgrim Century" were as simple and forthright as the plain but substantial frame houses of the period –a fitting background for the sparse, essential furniture that copied provincial English styles. The houses were usually made entirely of wood, and structural beams and posts were left visible in their natural wood coloring, a rustic contrast for the plain white plastered walls. Colors were brighter than is usually assumed, because anything still in existence has long since faded. Warm earthy tones that blended beautifully with natural woods were used almost as much as clear primary colors and that all-American combine of red, white and blue.

Here, red, white and blue adds color and sparkle to an Early American bedroom you could easily copy. (The mini-canopy is a cinch to make; directions follow.) Choose simple checks, plaids and floral patterns with a country feeling to complete the warm and informal Early American look.

ERNEST SILVA

16

The phrase "Early American" is commonly used to describe styles adapted from many different countries over a period of two hundred years. Much of the furniture and many of the accessories loosely labeled Early American are actually adaptations of European styles of the period; others are truly American firsts, such as the settle bench, predecessor of the modern Castro Convertible. This compendium makes no attempt to cover the whole spectrum of Early Americana; it does define and describe the most popular pieces much sought after today.

American Eagle

Since the choice of the eagle as the American patriotic symbol in 1782, it has been reproduced in wood, iron, earthenware, and china. The earliest ones in carved wood are among the most sought-after collectors' items.

Banjo Clock

A banjo-shaped wall clock devised in the 1790's by Simon Willard, now very much in demand by collectors.

Boston Rocker

A wood rocking chair with a high spindle back manufactured in New England in the early 18th Century. Back slat and front edge of the seat are decorated with stenciled designs.

Bull's-eye Mirror

A convex mirror with carved, gilded frame topped by an eagle, common in the late Colonial or Federal period.

Butterfly Table

A pine table with turned legs and swinging "wing" supports, corresponding in style to the gate-leg table of 17th-Century Jacobean England.

Collector's Guide to
EARLY AMERICANA

American Eagle

Banjo Clock

Boston Rocker

Bull's-eye Mirror

Butterfly Table

Carver Chair

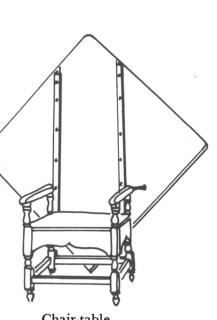

Chair-table

Corner Chairs

Corner Cupboard

Cottage Furniture

Carver Chair

A straight-back armchair of turned ash posts and spindles peculiar to the first settlements in the Massachusetts and Connecticut Colonies.

Chair-table

Literally a chair with a large round or square hinged back that turns into a table. Dating from the 1600's, it is particularly representative of the early settlers' functional furniture.

Corner Chair

A chair built to fit diagonally or catty-corner into a corner. The style dates from the late 17th Century.

Corner Cupboard

A triangular pine cupboard with upper shelves framed by a decorative three-sided cornice and a cabinet below.

Cottage Furniture

Painted pine furniture produced in volume in the late 1800's for a predominantly rural market. When it is stripped down to the natural wood, it bears a marked resemblance to the primitive Colonial style because of its simple lines and pine construction. Characteristic pieces are the dry sink and the lift-top commode.

Dry Sink

Hitchcock Fancy Chair

Dry Sink

Classified as cottage furniture, it once served the function of our kitchen sink. The sunken top was lined with galvanized tin to hold the dishpan or washtub, making it easily convertible to its present–day use as a bar or a decorative planter.

Fancy Chairs

Lightweight wood chairs produced in volume in the early 1800's. The name most often associated with this type is Lambert Hitchcock, the only manufacturer to label his chairs. Fancy chairs were always painted and decorated with stenciled gold leaf or bronze. Hitchcock chairs, decorated with copies of the original stencils, are still being produced in the original Hitchcock factory.

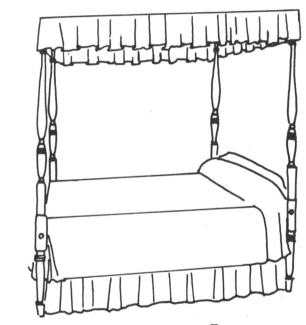

Four-poster

Four-poster

A large 18th-Century bed with four tall, turned posts at the corners to support draw curtains or a canopy.

Goddard Desk

An 18th-Century desk displaying concave and convex shell carving on each of the three sections of the block front. The block front refers to a center panel, recessed for leg room.

Goddard Desk

Hadley Chest

Hadley Chest

An oak or pine chest from the 1600's. The front is divided into three panels and carved, intaglio-fashion, with birds, leaves and arabesques.

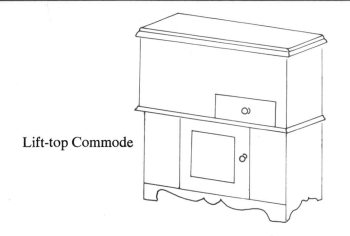

Lift-top Commode

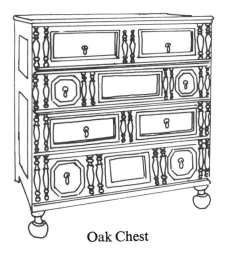

Oak Chest

Patchwork Quilting

Pennsylvania Dutch Chest

Pewter Teapot
and 8 inch Plate

Lift-top Commode

The best example of cottage furniture seen today, originally the counterpart of the modern bathroom. The top held a bowl and water pitcher, the drawer, soap and towels; the bottom was for other "temporary" storage.

Oak Chest

A low chest of drawers decorated with split spindles and raised molding around the drawers. The expert woodworking was typical of the New England cabinet makers of the 1600's.

Patchwork Quilting

The craft of sewing pieces of fabric together by means of seams. Whether rich or poor, all women of Colonial America practiced this craft and each colony had its distinctive geometric pattern. When the piece grew to the desired size, it was hand quilted onto a backing of cotton wadding.

Pennsylvania Dutch

Descriptive term for the whimsical furniture decorations and folk art of the German and Swiss immigrants to Pennsylvania in the 17th and 18th Centuries. Common motifs were hearts, flowers and birds stenciled or painted on chests, chairs and trunks.

Pewter

An alloy of tin and copper used in Colonial America for dinnerware. Characteristic pieces are the eight-inch plate, pitchers and teapots.

Pie Cupboard

A Pennsylvania Dutch cabinet for the storage of pies, consisting of a wooden cupboard with doors of perforated tin panels for ventilation.

Pudding Molds and Cookie Cutters

Classified as Country Antiques, these whimsically-shaped molds and cutters, once utilitarian, are now collectors' items. It was a Pennsylvania Dutch custom to decorate Christmas trees with cookies and cakes, resulting in a quaint collection of bird, beast and man-shaped molds and cutters.

Revere Silver

Elegantly simple silverware and bowls created by Paul Revere, a New England silversmith of the late 1700's. His punch bowl designed for the "Fifteen Sons of Liberty" is America's most famous piece of antique silver.

Salt Box

A small wooden box with lift-top lid decorated in the Pennsylvania Dutch style, originally hung on the kitchen wall to hold salt. A dough box is a bit larger and similarly decorated.

Sandwich Glass

Pressed glass developed in Sandwich, Massachusetts, in 1825. The method involved pressing molten gobs of glass into a mold with a plunger, resulting in smooth-edged patterns of eagles, stars, ships and crests.

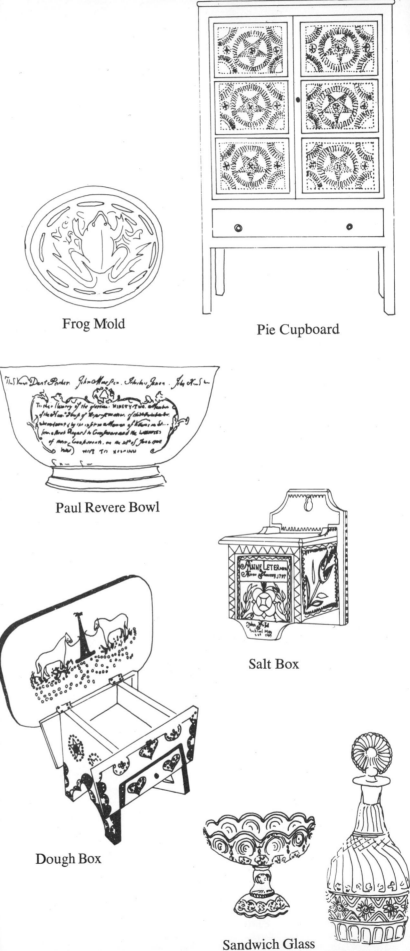

Frog Mold

Pie Cupboard

Paul Revere Bowl

Salt Box

Dough Box

Sandwich Glass

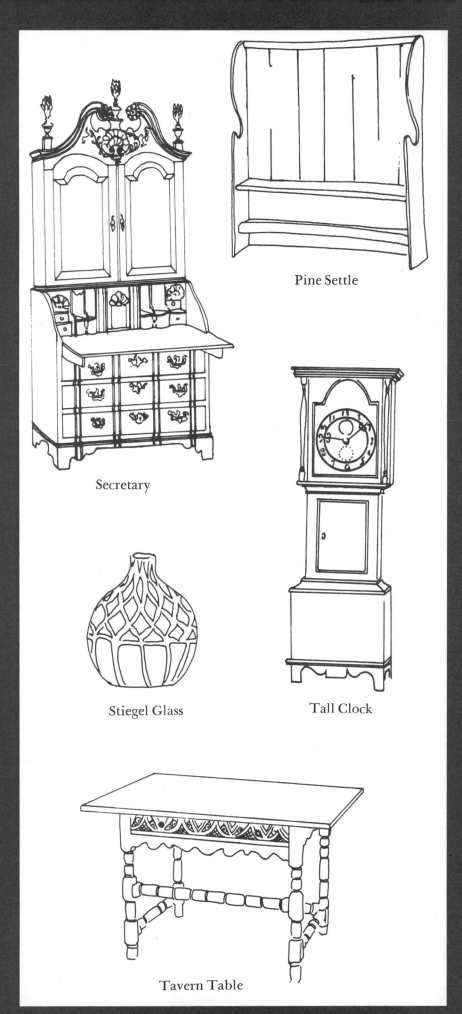

Pine Settle

Secretary

Stiegel Glass

Tall Clock

Tavern Table

Secretary

An 18th-Century slant-top desk with drawers below and bookcases above the writing area. Goddard carving and block-front construction gave it its traditionally American styling.

Settle

A high-back bench from the 17th Century with a narrow ledge-like seat made of broad pine planks. When the seat was unhooked and dropped forward, the settle converted into a bed.

Stiegel Glass

Glassware manufactured in the late 1700's with a characteristic diamond motif, usually tinted amber or blue.

Tall Clocks

Known now as "Grandfather" clocks, these late 17th-Century clocks resulted from the combined efforts of clock makers and cabinet makers. The lower section of the clock is a tall cabinet which encloses the pendulum.

Tavern Table

A rectangular table of the 17th Century with a pine top overhanging an oak or ash valanced frieze which is set upon turned legs and stretchers.

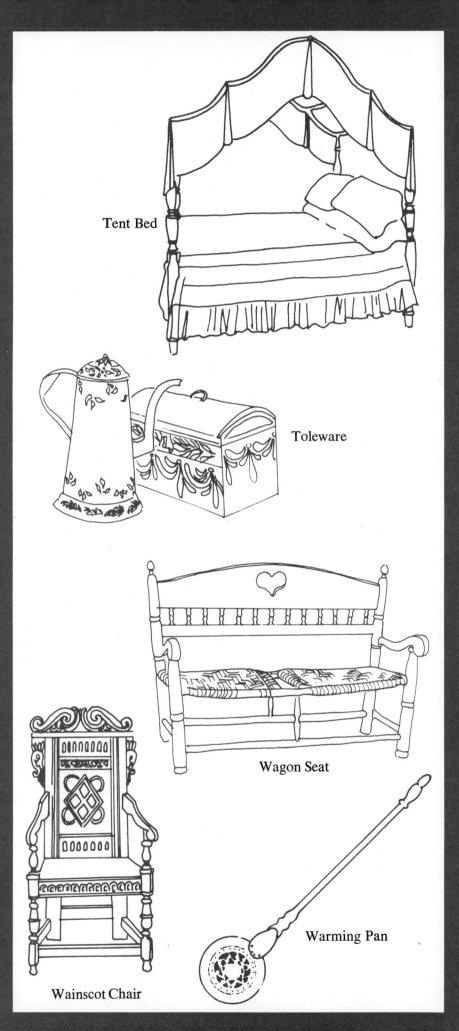

Tent Bed

Toleware

Wagon Seat

Wainscot Chair

Warming Pan

Tent Bed

Often referred to as a field bed, this 18th-Century bed has a tent-like canopy supported on four posts.

Toleware

Household articles made of painted or japanned tin. Tea caddies, trinket boxes and trays are painted with bright decorative motifs against a solid-color background, usually black.

Wagon Seat

A Pennsylvania Dutch wooden bench with rush seat and decorated back.

Wainscot Chair

Heavily carved oak arm chair dating from the 17th Century, corresponding to the English Jacobean style.

Warming Pan

A long-handled copper pan which was filled with heated coals and placed between the sheets to warm the bed.

Windsor Chair

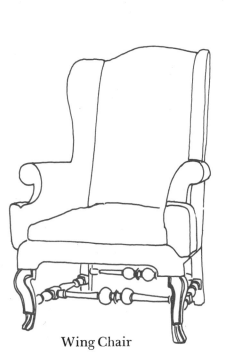

Wing Chair

Wooden Indian

Writing Chair

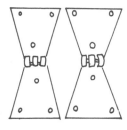

Butterfly Hinges

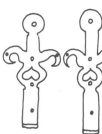

Open Heart Hinges

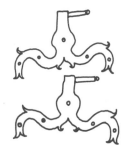

Staghorn Hinges

Windsor Chair

A style originated by English wheel-wrights who fitted spindles into the seat as they fitted spokes into a wheel. It became so popular in America that by the time of George Washington there were nine variations.

Wing Chair

Early 18th-Century easy chair with lateral wings, designed to shelter its user from drafts and capture the heat when placed before a fireplace.

Wooden Indians

Hand-carved and painted wooden Indians, once used to mark the location of cigar stores; now among the most-favored Early American memorabilia.

Writing Chair

Chair with large, flat right arm that served as a writing surface. Usually a Windsor style with spindle back.

Wrought-iron Findings

Decorative hinges, locks, latches and keys of black wrought iron, used extensively in Colonial America; now prized by collectors for their practical uses as well as antique worth.

HOW TO SLIPCOVER AN EARLY AMERICAN WING CHAIR

The easiest and most accurate method of making a slipcover is to pin and fit the fabric right on the chair. Working on one section at a time, place fabric against chair right side out to make pattern matching easy. Be sure length-wise grain of fabric is precisely vertical before pin-fitting each piece, and check again before cutting. Place fabric on each section so the pattern matches or blends well with the pattern on adjoining pieces. On a wing chair, center the design so the pattern continues from the inside back across the seat and down the front drop of the chair, and so inside wings and inside arms match and the fronts of the arms also match. If there is a cushion, the pattern on the top of the cushion should match the inside back of the chair. Outside arms and back do not have to match because they can't be seen at the same time.

When pin-fitting each section, mark seam lines along exact edge of chair (or section) with pins or chalk; when cutting, add 1″ extra on all sides of each piece for seam allowance. When placing welting on fabric, place stitching line of welting along edge of chair (or section), with seam allowance of welting to outside. The seam line on fabric and stitching line of welting will thus coincide; the slipcover will be stitched together along stitching line of welting. Baste all seams and try the slipcover on chair before final stitching so any alterations required for a smooth fit can be made at this point.

Start by placing fabric down inside back of chair and across seat, allowing 8″ for tuck-in between inside back and seat. Allow enough fabric along side edges of inside back to tuck in as far as possible between inside back and inside wings. Allow 4″ on each side of seat for tuck-in. Place welting along front edge of seat, clipping seam allowance to go around the corners. Stitch in place, following stitching line of welting. Place welting across upper edge of inside back; stitch in same manner. (See Diagram 1.)

Fit and cut fabric for inside wings, allowing extra fabric for tuck-ins where inside wings meet inside back. Fit and cut fabric for tops of arms.

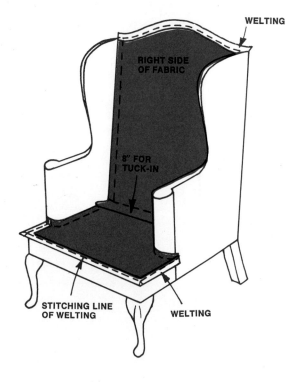

WELTING

RIGHT SIDE OF FABRIC

8″ FOR TUCK-IN

STITCHING LINE OF WELTING

WELTING

DIAGRAM 1

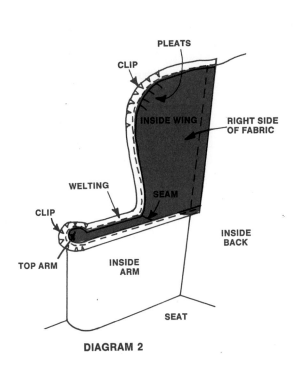

PLEATS

CLIP

INSIDE WING

RIGHT SIDE OF FABRIC

WELTING

CLIP

SEAM

INSIDE BACK

TOP ARM

INSIDE ARM

SEAT

DIAGRAM 2

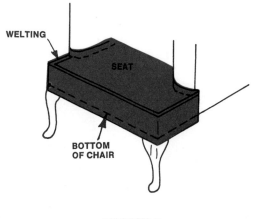

WELTING

SEAT

BOTTOM OF CHAIR

DIAGRAM 3

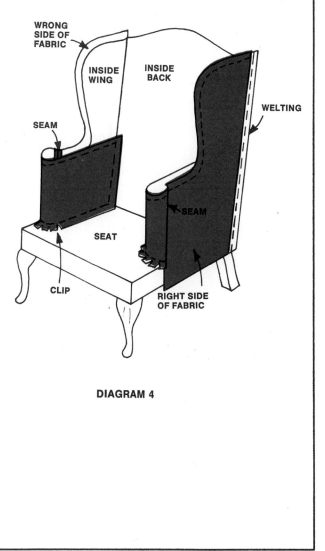

WRONG SIDE OF FABRIC

INSIDE WING

INSIDE BACK

WELTING

SEAM

SEAM

SEAT

CLIP

RIGHT SIDE OF FABRIC

DIAGRAM 4

Seam inside wings and tops of arms together where they meet. Place welting along lower edge of inside wing, around edge of arm, and up outside edge of wing to top of chair where inside wing meets inside back. Ease in extra fabric or make small pleats to allow for roundness of wing along the top curve. (See Diagram 2.) Repeat on other side.

Fit and cut fabric to cover front and side drop of seat. Stitch in place, following stitching line of welting already attached to front edge of seat. (See Diagram 3.)

Fit and cut fabric for outside wing and arm. Cut and fit fabric for inside arm, allowing for tuck-in where inside arm meets inside back, and allowing 5″ for tuck-in along bottom edge. Clip bottom edge to go around front curve of arm. Stitch arm sections together down outside arm as shown in Diagram 4. Attach welting to back edge of outside wing and arm. (See Diagram 4.) Repeat on other arm.

HOW TO
SLIPCOVER
A WING CHAIR

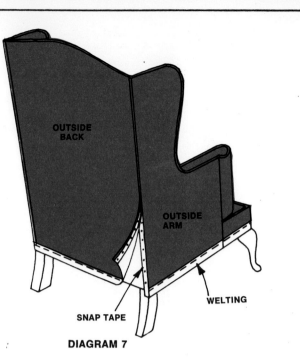

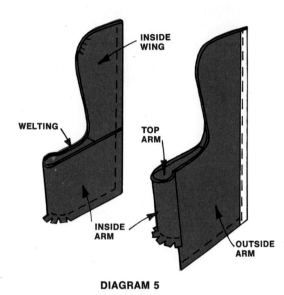

DIAGRAM 5

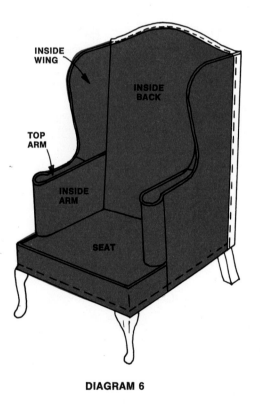

DIAGRAM 6

Stitch outside and inside wing and arm sections together, following stitching line of welting. (See Diagram 5.) Stitch lower edges of inside arms to seat. Stitch back (tuck-in) edges of inside arms to inside back. (See Diagram 6.)

Place fabric on outside back of chair and mark outline. Pin outside back to top of inside back and to outside wings. Try cover on chair, opening one side as much as necessary to place cover in position on chair. Make any necessary adjustments, then remove cover and stitch. Stitch snap tape or zipper to opening. Place welting around lower edge of chair (including back, sides and front), with stitching line of welting exactly at lower edge of chair. Stitch welting in place. (See Diagram 7.)

Cut under-seat flaps for sides 1″ longer than distance between front and back legs, and half the width of underside of chair. Make ½″ hems on both ends and along one side of each flap. Cut three 10″ lengths of ½″ twill tape and stitch to hemmed side of each flap for ties. Stitch flap to bottom of slipcover along each side, following stitching line of welting. (See Diagram 8.) Make front and back flaps in same manner. Put cover on chair; pull side flaps under chair and tie together. Turn seam allowance of welting under at corners; tie front and back flaps together.

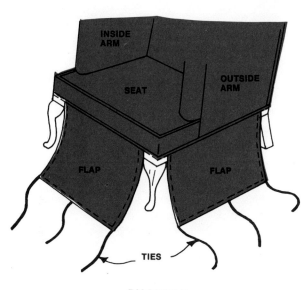

DIAGRAM 8

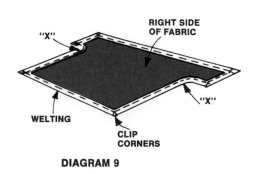

DIAGRAM 9

To cover cushion, place fabric on top, right side up, and pin welting around all edges. Clip seam allowance of welting to go around corners and curves. (See Diagram 9.) Trim fabric 1″ beyond stitching line of welting. Repeat for bottom of cushion.

Cut a boxing strip 2″ wider than depth of cushion and long enough to go around the front from the "X" mark on one side to the "X" mark on the other side, plus 2″. (See Diagram 9.) Cut two strips 2″ wider than one-half the depth of cushion and long enough to go around the back from "X" to "X", plus 2″. Fold 1″ under along one long side of each back strip. Place the two strips over the zipper with folded edges touching at center of zipper. Stitch along each side of zipper. (See Diagram 10.)

Taking 1″ seams, stitch front and back boxing strips together to form a complete circle. Place boxing strip on top section of cover, right sides together and raw edges flush. Stitch along stitching line of welting. (See Diagram 11.) Open zipper and attach other side of boxing strip to bottom section of cover in the same manner.

If your chair has a square or rectangular cushion, have zipper reach from the center of one side, around back to center of other side. Make boxing strips and attach in the same manner as above.

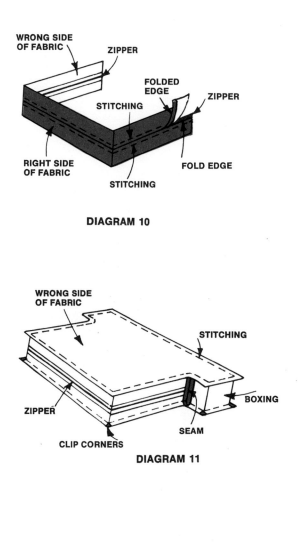

DIAGRAM 10

DIAGRAM 11

DIRECTIONS

FOR "EARLY AMERICAN" PROJECTS

BED CANOPY
AND DRAPERIES ON PAGE 14

MATERIALS NEEDED (for double bed):
- "1 x 2" clear pine: one 58½" for A, two 79¼" for B, one 60" for C
- Twelve 1¾" angle irons with ¾" and 1¾" flat head wood screws as required
- Two hollow-wall fasteners
- 2" finishing nails
- Fourteen yards snap tape
- 48" fabric and lining
- Staple gun and staples

NOTE: Canopy must be placed so 80" length will cross ceiling rafters.

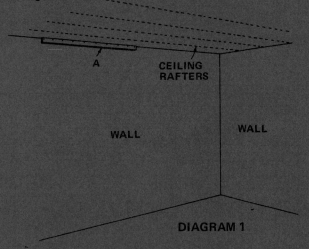

DIAGRAM 1

Nail A to wall at ceiling, spacing nails about 7" apart (Diagram 1).

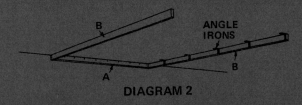

DIAGRAM 2

Using ¾" screws, attach angle irons to inside face of each B in positions corresponding to ceiling rafters. Nail B to each end of A and attach angle irons to ceiling with 1¾" screws (Diagram 2).

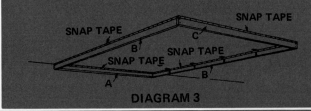

DIAGRAM 3

Attach two angle irons to inside face of C, spaced about 20" apart. Hold C in place and mark positions of hollow-wall fasteners on ceiling. Attach fasteners to ceiling and remove inner bolts. Nail C to B and replace bolts through angle irons into fasteners. Paint angle irons to match ceiling. Staple snap tape to inside faces of A, B and C at ceiling line, and to outside faces of B and C (Diagram 3).

DIAGRAM 4

Across full width of fabric, cut two pieces approximately 9½" to 10" deep (depending on design of fabric), cutting ½" outside design motif along lower edge. Seam two short ends together, matching fabric design; press seam open. Cut strip to 59½" length. Diagram 4 shows spacing for octagon-shaped design of fabric in photograph; adjust spacing to suit design of fabric used. Machine baste along bottom following edge of design motif.

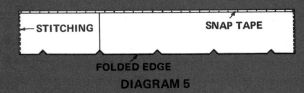

DIAGRAM 5

Cut an 81" length of lining fabric, then cut into four strips 81" long x same width as outer fabric. With right sides together, place strip of outer fabric on one strip of lining fabric so basting line on outer fabric falls on design line of lining fabric (if lining fabric is printed). Trim lining to match outer fabric and stitch together along bottom edge, following basting line; if notched or scalloped, clip into points for turning. Turn right side out and press bottom edge so fold is exactly along stitching line. Turn side and top edges in ½" and stitch close to edge. Stitch snap tape across top edge of outer fabric so snaps will match those of tape on inside of A (Diag. 5).

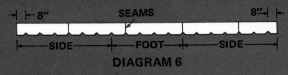

DIAGRAM 6

To make valance on other three sides: Cut strips of outer fabric and seam together as before until piece is 221" long and notches fall in positions shown in Diagram 6. There will be an 8" unnotched section at each end which will be against wall when finished.

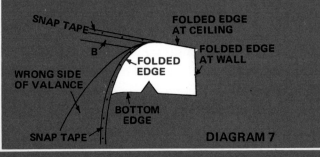

DIAGRAM 7

Cut one of the remaining lining strips to 61" and seam three strips together with ½" seams, placing 61" piece in the center. Press seams open. Machine-baste bottom edge of outer fabric, then attach to lining as before and turn right side out. Stitch snap tape along top edge of outer fabric on right side, making sure snaps on valance match those on outside faces of B and C, and allowing for ½" turn under at each end of strip. Turn snap tape to wrong side so fold is along edge of tape. Attach tape to outer faces of B and C (Diagram 7).

With outside of valance in place on B and C, mark positions of snaps on lining side, matching those on inside faces of B and C, so entire valance will hang straight. The inside corners of lining will have to be overlapped as inside of frame is shorter than outside measurements. Remove valance and stitch snap tape to top edge of right side of lining. Hang valance back in place. If side edge flares out at wall, attach a small ring to lower corner of valance and a cup hook to wall and hook valance in place.

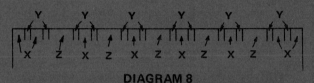

DIAGRAM 8

CORNER DRAPERIES:

Cut four lengths of outer fabric equal to distance from floor to ceiling, so complete design motif (in this case, the full octagon shape) ends at floor. Cut lining to same size. Place right sides together and stitch around side and bottom edges, ½" from edge. Turn right side out and press so seam is exactly along fold. Turn ½" at top of both fabrics to inside and baste across top edge. Mark spacing for pleats along top edge, having X equal 2", Y equal 1" and Z equal 4" (Diagram 8).

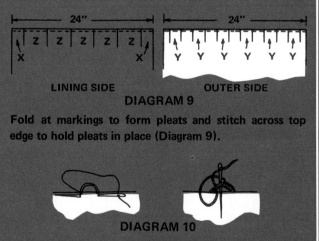

LINING SIDE   OUTER SIDE
DIAGRAM 9

Fold at markings to form pleats and stitch across top edge to hold pleats in place (Diagram 9).

DIAGRAM 10

Make a thread loop every 3" across top edge. To make loop, use buttonhole twist and sew two strands of thread to drapery, forming loop. Work over these strands with a blanket or buttonhole stitch (Diagram 10).

Attach small nails to inside of frame at corners in same positions as thread loops. Hang draperies in place with loops over nails.

BED CANOPY
ON PAGE 17

MATERIALS NEEDED:
(for 40"-wide unit)
 One " 1 x 10" x 40" pine for A
 One yard 44"-wide fabric (for canopy only)
 Three 3" angle irons with three ¾" and six 1¾" flat
  head wood screws
 Twenty-six ½" screw eyes
 ¾"-wide cardboard strips
 Staple gun and staples

Cut two 14½"-long pieces across full width of fabric so fabric design will match when 14½" ends are seamed together. Stitch the two pieces together, matching fabric horizontally and vertically. Press seam open. Cut piece to 63" width with seam in center. Turn ½" hem along each 14½" end. Along bottom edge, turn ½" to wrong side and then 1½" and blind-stitch hem in place.

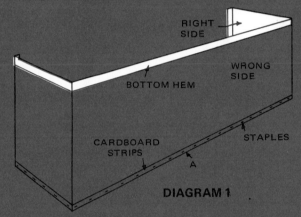

DIAGRAM 1

With right side of fabric against A, place top edge of fabric flush with bottom edge of A. Place cardboard strips on top of fabric with top edge of cardboard flush with top edge of A. Staple through cardboard strips and fabric into edges of A, as close to top as possible. Fabric will wrap around back edge of A 1½" on each side (Diagram 1).

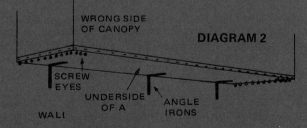

DIAGRAM 2

Locate three studs in wall at desired height; attach one angle iron to each stud with 1¾" screws. Attach ten screw eyes to bottom of A along each side edge and three at each front corner, placing them ½" in from edges and approximately 1" apart. Diagram 2 shows underside of canopy with fabric above it. Center A over the three angle irons, flush with wall (Diagram 2).

Screw through angle irons into A with ¾" screws. Attach drapery hooks to top edges of draperies and hang in place on screw eyes. Turn canopy down over edges of A.

HOW TO STENCIL FURNITURE

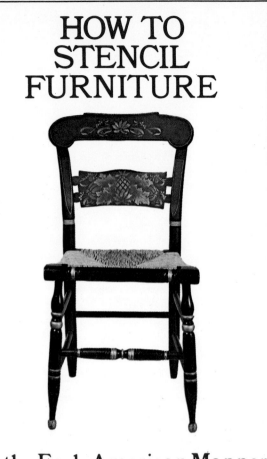

in the Early American Manner

Down through the ages, man has used painted decoration to embellish otherwise bland or uninteresting furniture and the Early American settlers were no exception. During the 17th and 18th Centuries, lacquered, or "japanned" furniture from the Orient was being widely imitated in Europe. The fashion, of course, spread to America, where the colonists came up with their own interpretation, creating an entirely new, refreshing style of decoration. Craftsmen trained in the art of japanning were attracted to the growing towns of Boston, Salem, New York and Philadelphia. Then, during the latter part of the 18th Century, the German or "Dutch" settlers in Pennsylvania created still another type of folk art by applying simple but gaily-colored designs to their relatively crude, country furniture.

The merging of these decorative styles resulted in the so-called "Fancy Chair," The Fancy Chair was a wooden side-chair or rocking-chair illuminated with beautifully hand-painted fruit and flowers. They were produced for the fine homes that were springing up all over New England. As the young country flourished, the production of furniture did the same. And as the small producers began to feel the effect of the larger factories, it was necessary to sacrifice the beautiful "free hand" decoration and substitute the much more rapid and economical stenciling technique.

The man most responsible for flooding the market with these lower-priced stenciled Fancy Chairs was Lambert Hitchcock. He manufactured chairs in parts and distributed do-it-yourself chair kits all over the country. Since he was the only manufacturer to sign his chairs, his name was preserved for posterity, and his originals have become collectors' items.

The actual practice of stenciling furniture lasted little more than a generation and was definitely not a home-practiced hobby. But the last thirty years have seen a revival of the craft by ambitious do-it-yourselfers who love the style but are loth to pay the high prices now asked for originals. Thanks to a small group of researchers and collectors, it is possible to obtain patterns of original stencil designs for chairs, chests, mirrors, clocks and many other pieces.

In its simplest form, the art of stenciling furniture is practiced by merely cutting a design into paper, placing the design over the piece of furniture and painting or dabbing the openings with metallic powder. The powder is applied to freshly varnished furniture, causing it to stick to the tacky surface. The design may be as simple or as intricate as your taste dictates and your talent allows, but the most beautiful designs are achieved with a gradual build-up of metallic powder and transparent colors. The bronze powder is applied first and then shaded with the transparent colors. The number of individual stencils involved depends upon the variety of motifs necessary to complete the design. For instance, a compote of fruit will require a stencil for each type of fruit as well as for the leaves and the compote. The designs on the Hitchcock chair opposite are composed of pineapple, melon, leaf and flower motifs shown in reduced size on Page 34. (Veins on large leaf to be painted in by hand.) Be sure to try a practice panel on plywood or cardboard before beginning your project.

Materials Needed:

Dry-cleaning fluid

Small piece of velvet

China plate to use as a palette

Turpentine (All brushes should be cleaned during painting sessions with turpentine and after each painting session with soap and water.)

½ pint can of oil-based flat black paint

½ pint can of Venetian red paint

Bronze powder

Artists' oils in alizarine crimson, burnt umber, Prussian blue, raw umber, cadmium yellow

2-inch bristle brush

Varnish brush

Several #2 square-tipped showcard brushes

Pointed camel's-hair brush for fine lines

20" x 50" sheet of acetate tracing paper

½ yard of architects' tracing linen

single-edge razor blades

9" x 12" window glass

Fine point pen and ink

Varnish

Step 1: Painting the background

If you plan to stencil an old chair which already has a build-up of layers of paint, it is best to strip it down to the natural wood before starting the project. On the other hand, if the surface is smooth, with no chipped or peeled areas, you can apply the paint directly over the existing coat.

Although Fancy Chairs were painted many different colors, the most common was black, with streaks of a red undercoat showing through, which gave the appearance of rosewood. For the undercoat, mix one part of Venetian red with one part of turpentine until it is the consistency of light cream. Using the 2-inch bristle brush, apply a thin, even coat of red and allow to dry overnight. Next, paint on a coat of flat black and while it is still wet, streak it so that some of the red will show through. This can be done with a stiff dry brush or a soft rag. The result will be brownish rather than black or red. Allow to dry overnight.

Step 2: Cutting the stencil

With acetate tracing paper, trace the design you are going to use from a pattern book (probably available at your library), or use our sample. (If you plan to re-use a design already on the chair, be sure to trace it before painting background.) You are now ready to trace the individual stencils on the architects' linen. This material is semi-transparent with one side glazed and the other matte-finished. The tracing is done on the dull side with pen and ink, keeping the lines as thin as possible. Since most stenciled designs are "built up", that is formed by overlapping motifs, you must make a separate stencil for each one. If the motifs are small you can place two on each sheet, but always leave a one-inch margin around each motif, in order to avoid staining surrounding areas with powder as you work. For the best protection, trace only one motif on each sheet, placing it in the center of the sheet. Number each stencil in the order that it is to be applied. For example, in our design, the pineapple fades as it reaches the leaf at the bottom, making it look as if it is overlapped by the leaf. Therefore, the leaf will be applied first, and when the pineapple stencil is placed over it, a portion of the leaf will show.

Cutting the stencil is a very delicate process and accuracy is required for a good result. Cut the motifs with a single-edge razor blade, using the window glass as a base. Cut just inside the tracing line, rotating the linen as you work. Make sure the cut lines meet exactly at corners to avoid "bleeding" of powders. Change blades as soon as both ends become dull.

Step 3: Make a layout tracing

Unless you are using the same design that was originally on the chair, it will be necessary to make a layout tracing. Start by tracing the outline of the slat you are going to decorate on acetate tracing paper. Using the original design as a model, arrange individual stencil motifs so that they will fit within slat outline. Now trace the various pieces in position within the outline of the slat, placing the tracing paper on top of your stencils. You will use this layout tracing as a gauge when you apply the stencils to the chair.

LAYOUT PATTERN (REDUCED) FOR CENTER SLAT, INDICATING AREAS TO BE SHADED.

LAYOUT PATTERN FOR TOP SLAT (REDUCED). USE MOTIFS 1 AND 6.

NOTE THAT MOTIF 6 HAS BEEN SPLIT INTO TWO PARTS.

HOW TO STENCIL
FURNITURE in the Early American Manner

Step 4: Applying bronze powder

Paint a smooth layer of varnish over the area of the chair to be decorated. Allow the varnish to dry long enough to achieve a tacky surface. The amount of drying time necessary will depend upon the moisture in the air. It usually takes an hour or two to reach the proper stage. Test with your fingertip . . . it should be sticky but not wet enough to allow finger prints.

You are now ready to apply the bronze powder. Pour a small mound of bronze powder onto your china palette and wrap and fasten a piece of velvet to the eraser end of a pencil, forming a bob. Place your first stencil in position, glazed side down, and hold it in place with your left hand. Pick up a tiny bit of the powder on the bob, and with a light circular motion, apply the powder to the tacky surface. Make sure all edges of the stencil are covered with powder. If you wish to shade or feather out the edge of the motif for an illusion of contour, or where it meets other motifs, use less powder where the design fades out. Apply a bit of pressure in the brighter areas of the unit to burnish them.

Now, with a dry brush, gently brush away all excess powder from the surface and from the stencil itself before lifting the stencil. Go on to the second stencil and apply bronze powder in the same manner. If the second motif is overlapped by the first, as in our sample design, feather the second motif as it meets the first. After using the stencils, remove all powder with dry-cleaning fluid. Never allow the architects' linen to come in contact with water, which will stretch and ruin the shape of the stencil. If a motif is repeated several times in one design, as is our third motif, you can use the same stencil as long as you clean it after each application of powder. Continue stenciling the pieces in their numerical order, feathering out to show contours and overlapping motifs. Allow powder to dry for twenty-four hours.

Step 5: Painting color overlays

Wipe the dry pattern with a damp sponge to remove any loose particles of bronze powder. Assemble your artists' oils, the china palette, showcard brushes, a quill brush, turpentine, varnish, and paint rags. It would be a good idea at this point to practice mixing colors to get the desired hues. First pour a small amount of varnish into a saucer; varnish will serve as the base for all transparent color mixtures. In addition to red, blue and yellow which you already have, you will be able to mix green (blue with yellow), orange (red with yellow), and purple (red with blue). Use the umbers to soften or tone down the colors and the varnish and turpentine to thin out the mixtures. Apply the colors to the appropriate motifs of the design in thin coats. You may want to shade the color just as the bronze powder is shaded. Do this by diluting the color with varnish. Indicate veining of leaves with full-strength color, using the camel's-hair brush. Allow the colors to dry for twenty-four hours and give the entire chair a coat of varnish.

Although we have stenciled our design on a Hitchcock chair, the technique of stencil decoration may be applied to any type of furniture. In fact, it was the custom in Early American times to stencil the walls and floors as well as the furniture! You may want to put traditional designs aside and start from scratch with your very own design. In any case, just remember that all it takes is a little time, a little patience, and above all . . . a steady hand. Before you know it, you will be producing a masterpiece. And don't forget to sign it . . . it *too* may become a collectors' item!

18Th-Century Colonial

emphasized comfort and elegance

GEORGE SMALL

The difference between Early American interiors and those of the more prosperous Colonial period is immediately discernible. As successful colonists engaged in commerce and trade accumulated wealth, austerity became a thing of the past, and gracious living prevailed — at least among the new aristocracy of the larger cities. Nowhere was this change more noticeable than in the flourishing city of Philadelphia, the furniture-making center of the colonies. By the time of the revolution, this Quaker stronghold was not only the largest, most populous colonial city, it was also – surprisingly – the leader in sophisticated living, a circumstance reflected in the design of "Philadelphia furniture." The rococo influence dominated, and the early Georgian and Chippendale styles were comfortable as well as elegant. This handsome living room, with its beautifully upholstered camel-back sofa and ornately carved chairs, is typical. Molding was usually recessed, but the same effect is achieved here with applied molding. More about this and making the Chinoiserie cornice follow this section.

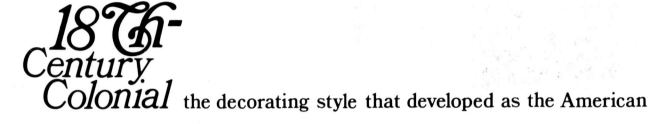

18th-Century Colonial the decorating style that developed as the American

Like fashion, the furniture and decorating styles of any era reflect the economic, political and social environment of their time. This is strikingly true of the style we call 18th-Century Colonial, which came into being as the initial struggle for survival in the New World gradually gave way to an economic boom and significant changes took place in the social environment of the New England colonies. The more adventurous spirits of the day continued their pioneering push westward, while the colonists who chose to settle permanently in the east pioneered in business and trade, both at home and with countries across the sea. Their endeavors prospered, and with prosperity the social order became stratified. An aristocracy of the middle class based on financial success emerged. Boston, Newport and Philadelphia became centers of commerce and trade–and therefore also of wealth. New European trade routes to the East inspired commerce and communication between the colonies, the continent, the Near East and the Orient. The delicate, whimsical flavor of the decorative arts of the East became a strong influence, introducing a refreshing change from the heavy, somber styles of the 17th Century.

While there had been little emigration from England during the latter years of the 17th

Century, the new prosperity attracted another wave of wayfarers from England and Scotland, among them many expert craftsmen, carpenters and cabinetmakers. So as the new colonial aristocracy accumulated wealth, artisans appeared who could satisfy their demands for more elaborate furniture and architecture copied from the current English styles. Indeed this burgeoning new class lived in much the same manner as many of their prosperous cousins across the sea, copying the English mode of dress and adopting English customs. These newly-elegant ladies and gentlemen wore satins and laces instead of puritanical homespun, and many had servants to serve their fine foods and wines. Coffee, tea and chocolate drinking became fashionable, and as the new affluence allowed more leisure time, parlor games became popular. Tilt-top, pie-crust and gallery-top tables for serving tea and coffee were widely used, and card tables, gaming tables, side chairs and settees appeared to accommodate the new social pastimes. There was a new emphasis on elegance and comfort in all the accoutrements of living. Chairs and settees were now stuffed, padded and upholstered. Luxurious fabrics were used freely in elaborate window treatments. The austerity of Early American bedrooms disappeared as highboys, lowboys, chests-on-chests and dressing

The Verplanck Room, 1763-67, with furnishings from the original residence at 3 Wall Street, New York; now in The American Wing of The Metropolitan Museum of Art

colonies prospered

tables came into use.

With these social and economic factors providing a receptive climate, the 18th-Century Colonial period, extending approximately from 1720 to 1776, introduced Georgian architecture and the furniture styles named for Queen Anne and Chippendale to the colonies. "Georgian" refers to the reigns of the first three English kings of that name, and the period is sometimes called "American Georgian."

GEORGIAN COLONIAL INTERIORS

The early settlers had all lived more or less alike, first in crude huts and later in modest wood dwellings, but as the colonies prospered, more formal, refined homes of wood, brick and stone were built by the new aristocracy. Dramatic entrance ways with spiral staircases appeared, and larger rooms and higher ceilings made the interiors more spacious. Decorative cornices, entablatures and pilasters in classic styles were applied to walls, fireplaces and windows. Walls were often divided into three parts–dado, middle section and cornice, with the dado alone or the dado and middle sector paneled. In paneling of this period, the panel was usually flush with the stile (the upright section of framing between the panels) and the moldings were recessed rather than applied. After 1735, the woodwork was often painted; the most popular colors were white, pearl, cream, grey-blue, mustard, brown and red. Marbling and graining were sometimes employed, and after wallpaper was first imported about 1737, scenic wallpapers from England and China were frequently applied to one or all walls above the dado. Stenciling of walls and floors became a popular form of decoration in less-pretentious homes where expensive wood paneling was not feasible. Fireplaces, usually constructed without a mantel shelf, were faced with marble, tile or bolection molding.

Window treatments were elaborate, with luxurious drapery crowned by all manner of swags, jabots, cascades and valances ornamented with fringe and tassels. Floor coverings ranged from fine carpets imported from France and the Orient to braided rag rugs produced at home.

COLONIAL FURNITURE

Although Queen Anne was neither interested nor influential in the development of the furniture style that bears her name, and Chippendale did not originate the style to which *his* name is universally applied, their names have become synonymous with 18th-Century Colonial furniture. Chronologically, the Queen Anne style came first, but the Chippendale style (which was derived from it) overlapped it to such a degree that the two are closely associated. The most important developments of the Queen Anne (and George I) period were the introduction of the curved line as an important element in furniture design; the first use of easily-carved mahogany as a cabinet wood; the adoption of Chinese motifs in furniture; and the extensive use of lacquer as a finish.

The hallmark of Queen Anne furniture is the cyma, or S-shaped curve, most noticeable in the cabriole leg, which first appeared with a "club foot," followed by the claw-and-ball form.

The splat-back chair, known also as the fiddle-back in America, is the most characteristic piece of furniture in the Queen Anne style. The solid back splat, echoing the graceful curves of a Chinese porcelain vase, was combined with cabriole legs and a broad seat. Later, the splat was pierced with simple, curved cut-outs and then with more elaborate designs, and carved shells or acanthus leaves were added to the "knee" of the leg and to the top of the splat. Solid wood or rush seats were used, but upholstered seats covered in damask, needlepoint or resist-dyed linen were more characteristic.

Other chairs of the period included the easy or wing chair with its entirely upholstered frame and side wings for protection from drafts; the corner-chair or roundabout with a low, quarter-circle seat; the armchair with upholstered seat and back; and finally, sofas or daybeds with upholstered seats. Couches as we know them today developed a little later with the Chippendale style.

Small round tables for serving tea and coffee had tilting tops set on tripods with cabriole legs. The typical pie-crust edge was designed for the practical purpose of keeping dishes from sliding off. Slightly larger round or rectangular tables for cards and other parlor games were sometimes constructed with compartments for holding cards and dice. Breakfast and dining tables had drop-leaf tops combined with shell-carved cabriole legs and claw-and-ball feet.

Highboys, lowboys, dressing tables, desks and secretaries all displayed characteristic legs, with shell carving on the drawers as well as on the legs. Corner cabinets and high chests with split pediments, used for storing fine china and ornaments, were decorated in the Oriental manner by a process known as japanning, which consisted of applying gold and enamel motifs to the lacquered wood.

It was during the Queen Anne period that framed mirrors – or "looking glasses" as they were called – were first imported and widely used in the colonies. Tall case clocks, or grandfather clocks, with cyma-curved frames replaced small wall clocks.

The furniture of the early Georgian period flowered from the simpler Queen Anne style, and the combination of graceful curves, the extensive use of rich mahogany, and the appeal

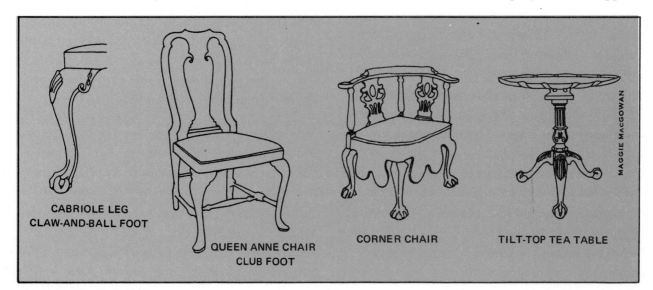

CABRIOLE LEG
CLAW-AND-BALL FOOT

QUEEN ANNE CHAIR
CLUB FOOT

CORNER CHAIR

TILT-TOP TEA TABLE

MAGGIE MACGOWAN

of more intricate carving all contribute to the general opinion that the second quarter of the 18th Century produced some of the finest furniture ever made.

The wide acceptance of the splat-back chair continued, but now the splat was elaborately pierced and carved. At the beginning of the Georgian era, the top of the chair took on the yoke-back form, with variations of the acanthus leaf and other foliage motifs substituted for the simpler shell carvings of the first quarter of the century. Wing chairs and other upholstered furniture became much more prevalent.

Then in 1754 the first edition of Thomas Chippendale's design book, "The Gentleman and Cabinet-Maker's Director" was published, and cabinetmakers in the colonies as well as in England had access to instructions for making the furniture designed by this most famous London furniture maker. The foremost experimenter and innovator of his time, Chippendale capitalized on the established trends in furniture design, borrowing from and refining the classic French, Chinese and Gothic forms, but always adding charming grace-notes of his own.

The Chippendale artistry is at its best in the chairs he designed, although he also produced furniture of every conceivable type. The cabriole leg with carved foot and the splat back with decorative yoke top were typical of his early work. Later he combined straight legs with intricate backs copied from Gothic tracery or carved into entwining ribbons (as in French rococo) or Chinese latticework or bamboo forms. He also produced chairs with gracefully curved ladder backs. The typical Chippendale sofa, described as "camel back" because of its curving, hump-like back, had an upholstered frame and square legs.

His designs in the Chinese manner are classified specifically as "Chinese Chippendale," and his fantastically elaborate mirror frames, combining French rococo forms with Chinese figures, are the outstanding examples of this style. The brass mounts and drawer pulls on Chippendale desks and chests also displayed ornate rococo curves. This rococo influence dominated the development of the Chippendale style in Philadelphia, with the "Philadelphia Highboy" a characteristic piece. But elements of the Queen Anne style, evident in the legs and shell carving of this still-popular tall chest, illustrate the overlapping of these two significant styles.

Chippendale designs varied all the way from florid rococo to severely classic. In his latter years, the classic influence dominated, and straight lines replaced the earlier Georgian style. His work of this period, produced in conjunction with the Adams brothers during the third quarter of the 18th Century, is generally considered his best. Because his work was so extensively copied, and his name used so indiscriminately, it is almost impossible to definitely identify specific pieces as having been made in his shop, and responsible authorities will do so only if the original bills of sale still exist.

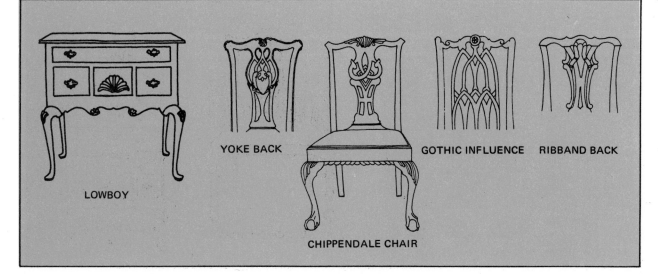

LOWBOY

YOKE BACK

CHIPPENDALE CHAIR

GOTHIC INFLUENCE

RIBBAND BACK

Other noted English cabinetmakers also published design books, and in their fervor to follow English fashions, the newly style-conscious colonists avidly bought up English books on architecture, interior decoration and furniture design. Those who could afford it imported English pieces; others relied on the cabinetmakers at hand to copy the desired designs. Many of these colonial cabinetmakers became remarkably adept at reproducing the Queen Anne, Georgian and Chippendale styles. Some of the best were located in Philadelphia, and have become famous for their "Philadelphia furniture." Not all of the pieces produced here and in other centers were direct copies, however. A Philadelphia version of the Windsor chair was made in many variations and manufactured in surprising quantities. Found in almost every 18th-Century household, these were also used in taverns and public institutions. Differing from the earlier English version, they were made primarily of spindles, without a central back splat, and with slender turned legs instead of the cabriole leg form. The rocking chair, a purely American innovation which was called a "nurse chair," developed from one form of the American Windsor, and rockers were soon applied to other types of chairs as well.

In Newport, too, noted cabinetmakers branched out to design furniture with individual characteristics. The work of three generations of Goddards and Townsends in this flourishing and cosmopolitan seaport includes some of the finest examples of American craftsmanship ever produced. Although they made many distinctive tables, chairs, urn stands and clock cases, they became most famous for their "block-front" desks, bookcases, cabinets and chests, with fronts divided into three vertical panels—the outer two convex, the center section concave. Elaborately carved shells adorned the top of each section.

Both the Philadelphia and Newport schools of design were strongly influenced by rococo forms which showed up in curved legs and steep scroll pediments. Touches of elegant carving, also French-inspired, were used for decoration.

The last quarter of the 18th Century saw furniture designs by Hepplewhite and Sheraton copied by colonial cabinetmakers as Queen Anne and Chippendale styles had been copied before them. George Hepplewhite, who in turn openly copied French furniture of the Louis XV and Louis XVI periods, was responsible for a newly delicate sense of line and proportion in English (and therefore colonial) furniture. As with Chippendale, his most typical pieces were chairs, always with slender, tapered legs. The backs of the chairs, in shield, camel, oval, heart or wheel shapes, had a delicate and airy effect achieved by delicate design rather than by carving. What ornamentation there was consisted of carved ribbons, fluting, reeding and festoons accented by wheat and vase motifs. The top rail of the shield back formed a serpentine curve, a line he used frequently in other types of furniture. Much of Hepplewhite's work was in

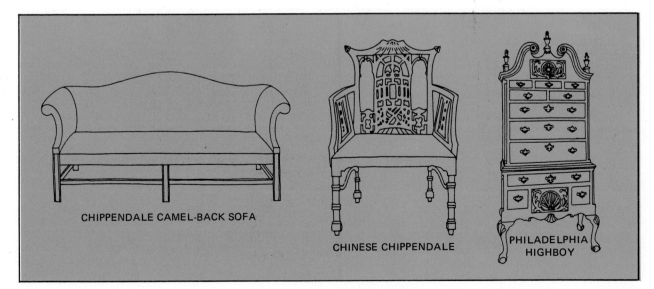

CHIPPENDALE CAMEL-BACK SOFA

CHINESE CHIPPENDALE

PHILADELPHIA HIGHBOY

satinwood, and he popularized painted motifs.

The third great English designer, Thomas Sheraton, published *his* design book in 1791, still in time to have tremendous influence on 18th-Century furniture. His chair legs were straight like those of Hepplewhite, but the straight line dominated his designs even more completely than those of his predecessor. His chair backs were rectangular in shape, with curves used only to connect straight lines or rectangular divisions. He did, however, use decorative center splats in the form of gracefully curved vases. Many of Sheraton's designs were highly original, and he was obviously intrigued with folding and multipurpose furniture. He used color and inlay more frequently than carving and was the first to use porcelain plaques for decoration. His linear forms found favor in the colonies as well as in England and are still a strong influence on contemporary design.

18TH-CENTURY ACCESSORIES

Unlike the early settlers, whose small furnishings were limited to purely functional accessories, the 18th-Century colonists profited from expanding trade with Europe and the Orient, and so had access to many additional niceties. In addition to silks and damasks, there was wallpaper from China and England, Oriental china for decorative as well as practical use, English china including Staffordshire and Wedgwood, and the blue and white Delft ware tiles from Holland, used frequently to decorate fireplace openings.

Painted or embroidered fire screens for protection from drafts and heat were decorative as well as functional, with tripod bases like those on the popular Queen Anne tea tables.

Although most of the colonial ceramics were imported from England, France and China, production of decorative glass was inaugurated in the colonies about 1760 by Baron Stiegel, a Pennsylvania German settler. This was clear blown glass with delicate, etched or enameled decoration. A cruder type of glass from New Jersey, known as "Wistarberg," was colored and bulbous in shape.

Pewter continued to be used for tableware as it had been in the 17th Century, but as the colonists became more affluent, the use of silverware increased. The designs were patterned after English pieces of the Queen Anne period, but American silversmiths tended to eliminate embellishment and concentrate on simplicity of line. Most famous of the colonial silversmiths was Paul Revere, whose designs for bowls, tankards, beakers and mugs are still being reproduced.

Lighting fixtures in the first part of the 18th Century were relatively crude candlesticks, candle stands and oil lamps made of wood, iron, tin and pewter. But as living became more luxurious and European furniture was imported in greater quantities, the colonists also imported fixtures from England and France in the form of bronze and marble candelabras, gilt and crystal sconces, and scroll-armed chandeliers.

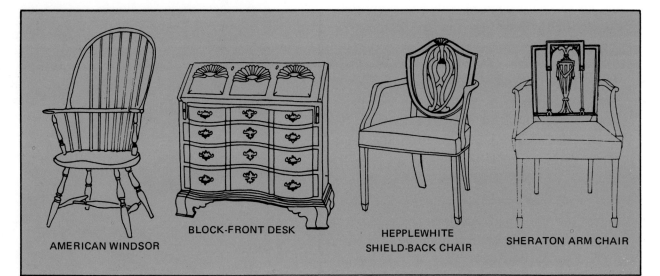

AMERICAN WINDSOR

BLOCK-FRONT DESK

HEPPLEWHITE
SHIELD-BACK CHAIR

SHERATON ARM CHAIR

18th-Century Colonial
signifies fine furniture design

The art of furniture making and decorative design reached a pinnacle during the 18th Century; in no other period of our history have the achievements in this field equaled those of the colonial cabinetmakers. This was the age of superb woodworking on both sides of the Atlantic, and while outright copying of Queen Anne and Chippendale designs was prevalent on both continents, variations within the styles were developed by several American schools of cabinetmaking. Isolated groups of artisans in the colonial towns and cities displayed great artistic independence, experimenting and improvising in an imaginative fashion. Among the regional styles of the period, the furniture made at Newport by three generations of Townsends and Goddards is unique in American craftsmanship. These meticulous Quaker cabinetmakers, closely related by intermarriage, became most famous for distinctive desks, bookcases, cabinets and chests in the *block-front* idiom. The fronts were divided into three vertical panels—the outer two convex, the center one concave, and all three surmounted with big, exquisitely-carved shells, these also concave and convex.

Pièce de résistance of the room at the right, with typical recessed window and paneled woodwork, is the authentic reproduction of a block-front Townsend chest, with characteristic trio of beautifully-carved shells. Chairs and tables in the Queen Anne style were also made by the Townsends in Newport, so a room furnished entirely with their masterpieces might have looked much like this. Directions for making the scalloped cornice, so much in keeping with the graceful curves of the period, follow this section.

GEORGE SMALL

HANS VAN NES

Fine furniture was also much in evidence in 18th-Century Williamsburg, the capital of Virginia and probably the gayest spot in the colonies. The great Tidewater plantations were the ultimate in colonial affluence, and the owners lived like their monied English cousins, importing English furniture and also acquiring the best that Philadelphia and New England had to offer. Much of it was undoubtedly in the Queen Anne style, the chairs with typical urn-shaped splats and cabriole legs like those above, which also indicate the evolving yoke back.

45

18th-Century Colonial

is at its best in a setting of classic symmetry

18th-Century Colonial furniture was essentially gracious in character, with a pleasant degree of formality that was neither pretentious nor cold. Imported from England via sailing ships or produced in the colonies by skilled artisans and craftsmen, it graced fine town houses in the North and affluent plantation homes in the South, where life was leisurely but well-ordered, comfortable but never casual. That is why even today, and even in smaller, less-formal settings, furniture with a Colonial heritage is most at home in a balanced, traditional arrangement, as in the dining room seen here. In a prosperous 18th-Century home, the dining room itself would probably have been larger, with a loftier ceiling. But the windows would have been symmetrical and festooned with fringed swags and cascades in much this same manner. Directions for making the swagged valances shown follow this section.

46

HANS VAN NES

18th-Century Colonial
combines beautifully with crewel-patterned fabrics

The fabrics used for draperies and upholstery in the large and affluent homes of Colonial America were often luxurious damasks in rich golds, subtle greens and glowing reds. Velvets, taffetas and other silks were imported in great quantities from France, England, Italy and even Spain and Portugal. But less elaborate fabrics in scenic designs, floral patterns and printed *toiles* were also popular. Needlecraft was a major preoccupation of the fairer sex, and the passion for crewel embroidery that began in the "pilgrim century" continued unabated. Here you see how a contemporary adaptation of a crewel pattern adds liveliness and color to a traditional fireside setting that features twin Chippendale-style sofas in a symmetrical arrangement. The fabric used to cover the sofas and the tailored cornices is quilted–a luxurious touch that adds considerably to the warm and comfortable look of this inviting room. Attractive crewel-patterned fabrics abound today; with luck, you may find one that comes both quilted and unquilted. If not, this charming effect is well worth quilting your own. Directions for making the cornices follow.

As the new-found prosperity of the 18th Century gradually replaced the early struggle for survival, life in the colonies became more leisurely and comfortable – even luxurious for members of the new aristocracy who reaped the benefits of increasing commerce and trade. Homes and their furnishings quickly reflected the more affluent life style, and the change was perhaps more marked in the bedrooms than anywhere else. The crude four-poster beds which had been swathed in drapery for warmth gave way to elegant arched or flat-topped tester beds with turned and carved posts topped by decorative finials. Where the only other furniture had been a utilitarian chest or two, highboys, lowboys, dressing tables and comfortable chairs for reading and relaxing now appeared. The room at the right, splashed with charming Chinoiserie, re-creates the gracious mood of an 18th-Century bedroom, and you can do the same. Turn to Page 54 to learn how to "panel" walls the easy way, and find directions and diagrams for making the bed canopy, coverlet and dust ruffle a few pages further on.

18th-Century Colonial

inspires a gracious
and relaxing bedroom

GLOSSARY
OF 18th-CENTURY DECORATING TERMS

Architrave: *The lowest, horizontal section of the three main parts of the classical entablature, immediately above the capitals of the columns and below the frieze. The term is also used to define moldings used in a similar way as door or window trimming.*

Bandy Leg: *Lay term for cabriole leg with club foot. It preceded the cabriole leg with claw-and-ball foot in 18th-Century furniture.*

Bolection Molding: *Molding which projects sharply beyond the woodwork or wall to which it is applied (usually into the room). In the 18th Century it was frequently used as a fireplace trimming in lieu of a mantel shelf.*

Cabriole Leg: *A cyma-curved furniture leg designed in the form of a stylized animal's leg with knee, ankle and ornamental foot.*

Case Clock: *A clock with its works enclosed in a tall case. In the Queen Anne period, large case clocks replaced small wall clocks. Also called grandfather clocks in the colonies.*

Claw-and-Ball Foot: *A type of carved foot used with the cabriole furniture leg. It consists of a bird's claw grasping a ball. Introduced in early 18th Century England (after the club foot). Possibly of Oriental origin.*

Club Foot: *A foot used on the cabriole leg in early 18th-Century furniture. The foot flares into a flat, rounded form which rests on the floor. Sometimes called a pad foot.*

Cornice: *In classical architecture, the topmost, projecting section of the three main parts of the entablature. Often used on interior walls without the lower two sections. Now also a term for the decorative band at the top of a window that conceals drapery hardware.*

Cyma Curve: *A graceful, S-shaped curve which was the main hallmark of Queen Anne furniture.*

Dado: *Term for the lower section of a wall, when treated differently from the surface above it. Usually topped with crowning or cap molding, which was sometimes called a chair rail.*

Decalcomania: *A form of decoration in which printed designs on thin, specially-treated paper are transferred onto other materials. An extremely popular and fashionable hobby as well as a technique used by professionals to decorate furniture during the 18th Century.*

Entablature: *In classical architecture, the portion of the order supported by the column, consisting of the architrave, frieze and cornice. Also the upper section of a wall.*

Fiddle-Back Chair: *An American Colonial, rush-seated chair in Queen Anne style. Solid back splat approximated a fiddle-back or vase shape. Called a splat-back chair in England.*

Frieze: *The middle, horizontal section of the three main parts of the classical entablature. Usually a flat surface decorated with ornamental features or with carving. Often used on interior walls without the architrave or cornice.*

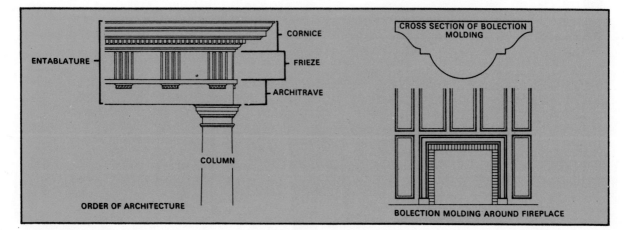

Gallery: *A miniature railing, either pierced or solid, along the edge of a table top or a shelf. Specifically, a gallery-top table.*

Highboy: *A tall chest of drawers on a table-like base or a lowboy. In the 18th Century, it was usually designed with either a flat molded top or a scrolled pediment top.*

Japanning: *A process used extensively in the 18th Century in which metalwork and furniture were completely covered with colored lacquer and the decoration raised and painted with gold and colors. Many ornamental motifs were used, including foliated scrollwork and pseudo-Chinese motifs. Amateur japanning became a fashionable hobby during this period.*

Lowboy: *A side table with drawers, standing approximately three feet high. It was frequently decorated with quarter-round, fluted stiles and carved with recessed shell motifs. In England, it was known as a dressing table.*

Order: *A style of building. In classical architecture, a type of column and entablature considered the definitive unit of a style. For example, there were three major Greek orders, or styles: Doric, Ionic and Corinthian.*

Pediment: *Originally, the triangular space forming the gable on each end of a Greek temple. In 18th Century furniture, an ornamental feature at the top of highboys and secretaries, generally triangular in shape but broken or segmented in decoratively carved forms.*

Piecrust Edge: *The upstanding edge of a small, round table carved or molded in scallops. Used especially on revolving, tilt-top tables.*

Pilaster: *A flat, vertical wall projection, or false column, with the general proportions and the same divisions (capital, shaft and base) as a free-standing column. Popular as a wall treatment during the late 18th Century.*

Rails: *In wall paneling, the horizontal strips of the frame, used to separate the panels.*

Resist-Dying: *A method of drying fabric in which the pattern area is covered with a chemical paste or paraffin. When the cloth is dyed, the covered parts resist the dye and retain their original color. In the 18th Century, resist-dyed linen was commonly used to cover chair seats.*

Roundabout Chair: *Chair designed to fit into a corner, with a low back on two adjoining sides of a square seat. Also called a corner chair.*

Secretary: *A tall writing desk, especially one in which the top section was used for books.*

Settee: *A long seat or medium-sized sofa with a high back, seating several persons.*

Shell Carving: *Carving in the form of a shell, a typical design motif used in the 18th Century to ornament the knees of cabriole legs, the tops of chair splats and other furniture.*

Stenciling: *A method of decorating or printing a design on a surface by brushing ink or dye through a cut-out pattern. Employed to decorate both walls and floors in small houses where wood paneling and rugs were not used.*

Stiles: *In wall paneling, the vertical strips of the frame, used to separate the panels.*

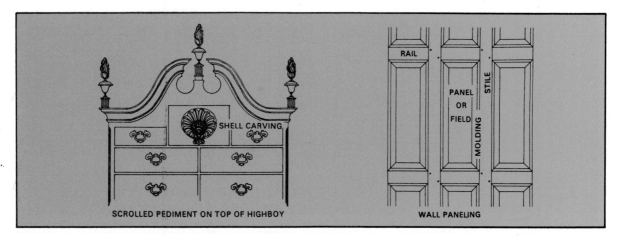

SHELL CARVING

SCROLLED PEDIMENT ON TOP OF HIGHBOY

RAIL

PANEL OR FIELD

MOLDING

STILE

WALL PANELING

HOW TO HAVE THE 18th-CENTURY LOOK OF PANELED WALLS

Wood paneling has been used in all period styles, and few other types of wall decoration have such warmth and charm. The insulation of wood-lined walls is no longer necessary, but the decorative look of paneling is often desirable, particularly in rooms with an 18th-Century ambiance. In paneling of that period, the panel was usually flush with the vertical section of the frame called the *stile,* and the moldings were recessed. But the cost of this kind of cabinetry is practically prohibitive today, and the same effect can be achieved with *applied* molding. This method was used in the room settings we designed to show you how to achieve the 18th-Century Colonial look, and the detail drawings below show profiles of the specific moldings involved and how they were used.

Stock moldings are available in an amazing variety of shapes, and in lengths from three to sixteen feet. When measuring the lengths of molding required, always round off the measurement to the next highest foot. Note the number of pieces you need in each length and pattern, and your lumber dealer will supply random standard lengths from which you (or he) can cut the lengths you require with the least waste. When measuring moldings which are to be mitered, add the width of the molding to the length for each miter. If the length is to be mitered at both ends, double the width of the molding and then add that amount to the length.

The numbers of the moldings noted in the drawings are those used by Le Noble Lumber Company, 522 West 52nd Street, New York City, but they are all standard stock moldings and should be available at any well-stocked lumber yard in your own area.

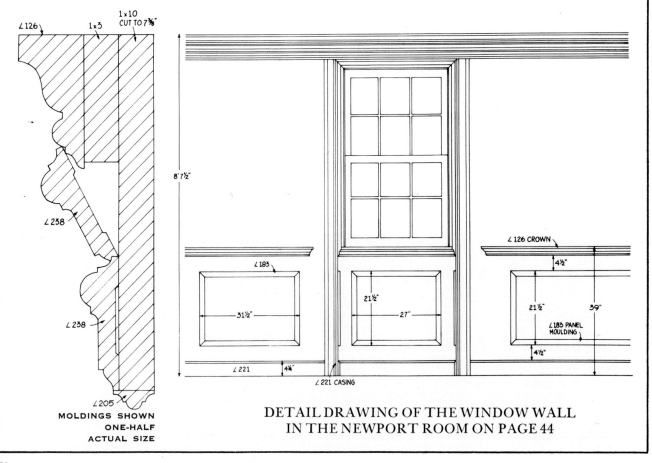

MOLDINGS SHOWN
ONE-HALF
ACTUAL SIZE

DETAIL DRAWING OF THE WINDOW WALL
IN THE NEWPORT ROOM ON PAGE 44

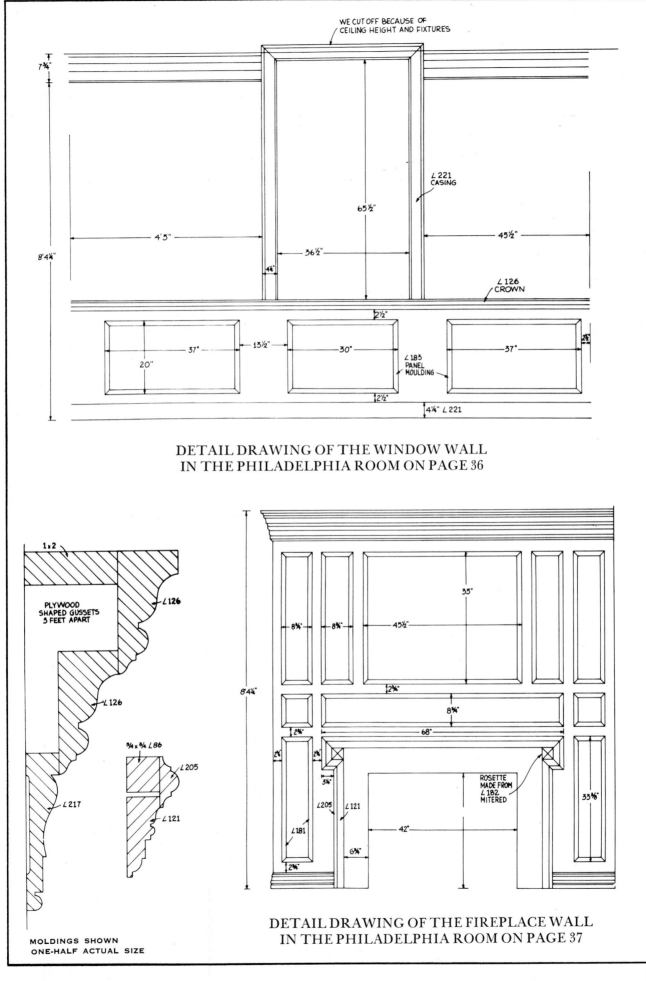

WE CUT OFF BECAUSE OF
CEILING HEIGHT AND FIXTURES

7¾"

8'4¼"

65½"

∠ 221
CASING

4'5"

45½"

36½"

4¼"

∠ 126
CROWN

2½"

37"

13½"

30"

37"

2½"

20"

∠ 183
PANEL
MOULDING

2½"

4¼" ∠ 221

DETAIL DRAWING OF THE WINDOW WALL
IN THE PHILADELPHIA ROOM ON PAGE 36

1 x 2

PLYWOOD
SHAPED GUSSETS
5 FEET APART

∠ 126

∠ 126

¾ x ¾ ∠ 86

∠ 205

∠ 121

∠ 217

35"

8¾"

8¾"

45½"

2¾"

8¾"

68"

2¾"

2¼"

2¼"

3¼"

ROSETTE
MADE FROM
∠ 182
MITERED

33⅝"

8'4¼"

∠ 205

∠ 121

∠ 181

42"

6¾"

2¾"

MOLDINGS SHOWN
ONE-HALF ACTUAL SIZE

DETAIL DRAWING OF THE FIREPLACE WALL
IN THE PHILADELPHIA ROOM ON PAGE 37

DIRECTIONS
FOR "18th-CENTURY COLONIAL" PROJECTS

CHINOISERIE CORNICE
ON PAGE 36

MATERIALS NEEDED:
(for 43" window)

One ⅜" x 14" x 54" plywood for A
Two "1 x 4" x 10" pine for B
One "1 x 4" x 49½" pine for C
Two 2½" angle irons with two ⅝" screws and four 1¾" flat head wood screws
1¾ yards of fabric
2¾ yards of tasseled trimming
4½ yards of ¾"-wide flat gold braid
4 yards of ½"-wide flat gold braid
1½" common nails
Household cement
Staple gun and staples
Tissue paper
Dressmaker's tracing paper
Tracing wheel

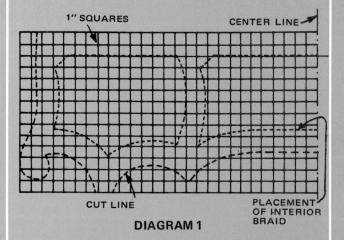

DIAGRAM 1

Mark 1" squares on A. Using Diagram 1 as a guide, enlarge outline of A and pattern for placement of interior braid. Trace both onto tissue paper and set aside. Cut A along outside outline.

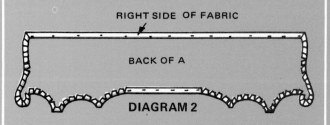

DIAGRAM 2

Cut fabric to 18" x 63" and place A in center of wrong side of fabric. Wrap fabric over top edge and staple to back of A. Pull fabric around side and lower edges,

clipping and easing where necessary to go around curves. Staple to back of A so fabric is smooth on front (Diagram 2).

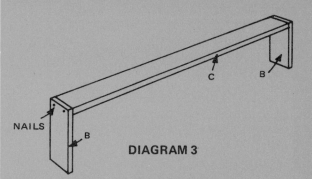

DIAGRAM 3

Using two nails at each end, attach one B to each end of C (Diagram 3).

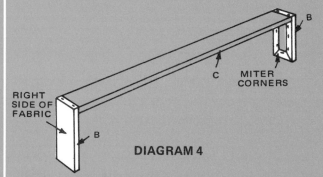

DIAGRAM 4

Cover outside face and bottom edge of each B with fabric, mitering corners smoothly and stapling to inside face of B and top of C (Diagram 4).

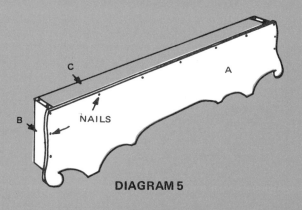

DIAGRAM 5

Center A on B and C with top edge of A flush with top face of C; nail through A into C, spacing nails about 9" apart. Nail through A into B with 3 nails on each side. When nailing A to B and C, make sure nail heads are no more than ¾" in from edge of A so they will be covered by braid (Diagram 5).

Glue tasseled trimming down each side and along lower edge so tassels hang free, holding trimming in place with pins or thumb tacks until glue has dried. Glue ¾" braid over tape of tasseled trimming and continue along top edge. Using the tissue paper pattern, dressmaker's tracing paper and a tracing wheel, transfer pattern for the placement of interior braid to fabric covering front of A. Glue ½" braid to front of A, following this pattern.

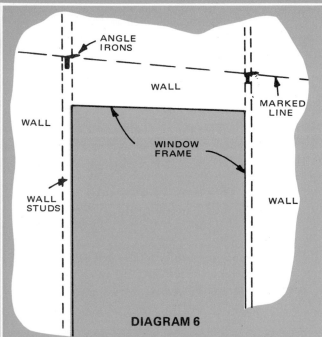

DIAGRAM 6

Hold cornice in desired position over window and mark underside of C on wall. Attach one angle iron at each side of window so top of angle is on marked line, screwing into wall studs with two 1¾" screws for each angle iron (Diagram 6). If cornice is to be hung flush against ceiling, place tops of angle irons ¾" down from ceiling and remove molding at ceiling line.

Place cornice on angle irons and hold in place with a ⅝" screw through each angle iron into underside of C.

SCALLOPED CORNICE
FOR RECESSED WINDOW ON PAGE 45

MATERIALS NEEDED:

Fabric required (depending on width of window)
One piece of pine, "1 x 12" × required length for A
Two "1 x 2" x 12" pine for B
Six 1½" flat head wood screws
Four 3" mending plates with eight ⅝" and four 1¾" flat head wood screws
2"-wide fringe, ½"-wide flat brown tape and ½"-wide flat green tape as required
Padding
Staple gun and staples
Household cement

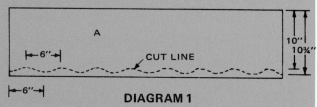

DIAGRAM 1

Draw scalloped design on "1 x 12" for A as shown in Diagram 1. Cut along scalloped line with jig saw. Scallops do not have to be perfect; fringe will cover edge.

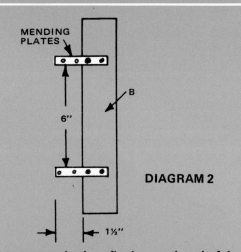

DIAGRAM 2

Cut B to correct depth to fit along each end of A so B will be flush with top and bottom edges of A. Attach two mending plates to each B, 2" from each end, using two ⅝" screws in each plate (Diagram 2).

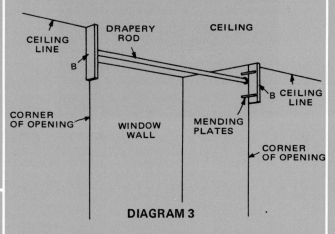

DIAGRAM 3

Hold B in place at each side of opening and against ceiling. Mark position of one hole in each mending plate on wall. Drill a pilot hole at each position for a 1¾" screw (Diagram 3).

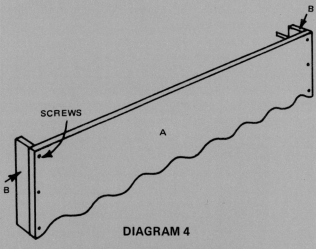

DIAGRAM 4

Drill three pilot holes at each end of A, placing them ⅜" in from ends, 1" from top and bottom edges and one at center of depth. Screw through holes with 1½" screws into center of thickness of each B so end of A is flush with outside face of B (Diagram 4).

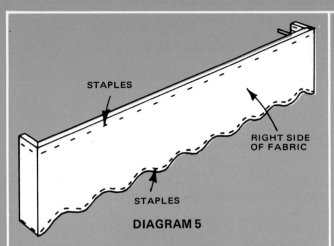

DIAGRAM 5

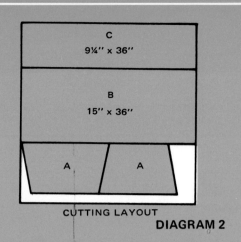

CUTTING LAYOUT

DIAGRAM 2

Place padding over front of A and cut along curved lower edge. Place fabric over padding so design is straight across top edge of A. Pull fabric around each end and staple to inside of B, clipping to go around mending plates. Smooth fabric over top edge and staple to inside of A and B, mitering corners. Trim fabric along lower edge and staple in place. Place a line of staples along top 1" from edge (Diagram 5).

Staple fringe along scalloped lower edge, then glue flat green tape over tape of fringe. Cover top row of staples by glueing flat brown tape in place. Hold tape in place with pins or thumb tacks until glue has set (see photo).

Hang cornice in position with a screw through each mending plate into previously drilled pilot holes.

From plywood, cut two A to size and shape shown in Diagram 1; one B, 15" x 36"; one C, 9¼" x 36". For cutting layout, see Diagram 2.

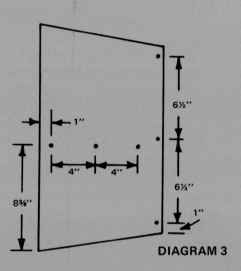

DIAGRAM 3

SHIRRED CORNICE
ON PAGE 45

MATERIALS NEEDED:
(for each 30" window)
- ¾" x 36" x 36" plywood
- Twelve 1½" flat head wood screws
- Two yards 48"-wide fabric
- Two 2½" angle irons with two ⅝" and four 1¾" flat head wood screws
- Six 1½" common nails
- Staple gun and staples
- Paint

Drill six pilot holes for screws in each A in positions shown in Diagram 3. The three holes along the 15" sides should be ⅜" in from edge.

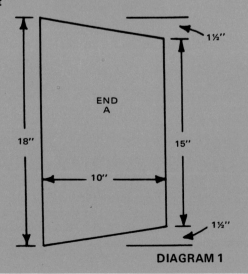

DIAGRAM 1

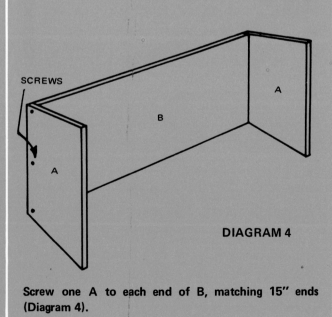

DIAGRAM 4

Screw one A to each end of B, matching 15" ends (Diagram 4).

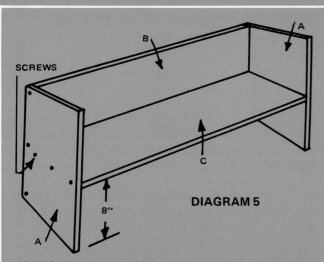

DIAGRAM 5

Attach C with three screws through each A into center of thickness of C. On outside of B, draw a line 6⅞" from lower edge and nail through B into C on this line with nails spaced about 6" apart (Diagram 5).

Paint undersides of A, B and C to match wall as they may be visible when draperies are open.

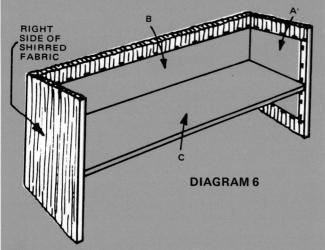

DIAGRAM 6

Cut fabric into three 24" x 48" pieces. Taking ½" seams, seam together along 24" edges to form one long piece 24" x 142". Run two rows of gathering stitches along each 142" side, 2" from each raw edge. Place fabric over cornice and pull up gathering stitches until fabric is the correct length to fit around the entire cornice and extend 2" onto the back of each A. Staple to back of each A, cutting fabric to go around C. Adjust gathers so folds are even; turn fabric over top edge and staple to insides of A and B. Repeat along lower edge (Diag. 6).

Before hanging cornice, install casement and drapery rods. Attach regular curtain rods to window frame and hang casement curtains. Use 7" projection brackets to hold drapery rod away from wall. Extra space between rod and inside of B is necessary to permit draperies to be opened. Hang draperies on rod and across brackets to wall (see photo).

Hang cornice in place in same manner described for chinoiserie cornice on Page 57, Diagram 6. Place angle irons so lower edge of B will cover top of draperies by 2 or 3 inches. Paint angle irons to match wall.

SWAGGED VALANCES
ON PAGES 46–47

MATERIALS NEEDED (for two 40" wide windows):
    Four yards of 54" wide fabric
    7½ yards of tassel trimming
    Two "1 x 4" pine x 45"
    Six 2½" angle irons with ¾" and 1¾" flat head wood
      screws
    Upholsterers' tacks or staple gun and staples

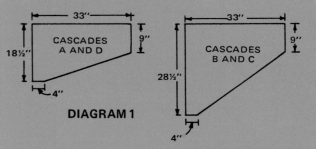

DIAGRAM 1

Cut paper patterns for side cascades to dimensions shown in Diagram 1.

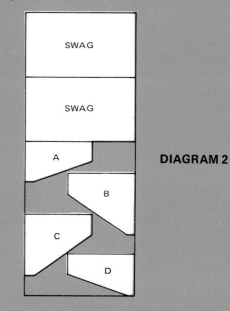

DIAGRAM 2

Cut two swags 36" x full width of fabric. Cut cascades A and C. Reverse patterns and cut cascades B and D (Diagram 2).

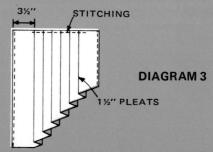

DIAGRAM 3

CASCADES:
Make a ¼" hem down side edges of A. Starting 3½" from left edge, make 1½" pleats across width, then stitch across top, ½" from edge, to hold pleats in place (Diagram 3).

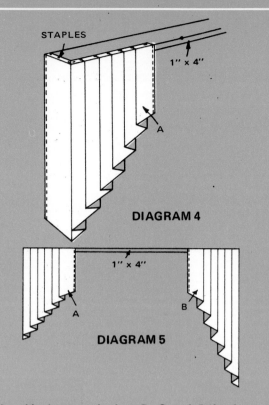

DIAGRAM 4

DIAGRAM 5

Make side hems and pleat B, C and D in the same manner, with pleats in C going in same direction as in A and pleats in B and D going in the opposite direction. A and B are for right-hand window; C and D are for left-hand window (see photo).

Turn ¼" to wrong side of fabric along lower edges of A, B, C and D and place edge on tassel trimming. Stitch along edge through fabric and trimming. (Tassel trimming is not shown on diagrams in order to show direction of pleats.)

Staple A to left end of "1 x 4" as shown in Diagram 4, with ½" of fabric along top edge of board. Attach B to right end of "1 x 4" in same manner, as shown in Diagram 5.

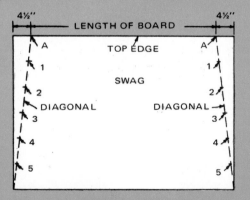

DIAGRAM 6

SWAGS:

Mark points A 4½" in from each side along top edge. If length of board is more than 45" it will be necessary to seam fabric to make it 9" wider than length of board. Draw a diagonal line from point A to lower corner on each side. Divide diagonal line into six equal parts and mark points 1 through 5 along each line (Diagram 6).

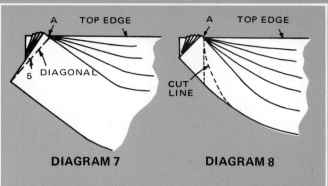

DIAGRAM 7   DIAGRAM 8

Pin swag to back of a couch so top edge is straight and swag hangs down. Pin point 1 to A at each side, smoothing in fold from center to sides. Pin point 2 to A, then 3 to A, etc. (Diagram 7).

When all points are pinned to A, cut off excess fabric on both sides. First cut straight down from point A, then cut in curve to bottom edge to form lower edge of swag (Diagram 8). Stitch tassel trimming along lower edge in same manner as for cascades. Place swag on board and staple in position so folds hang in desired positions.

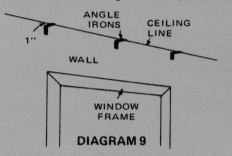

DIAGRAM 9

Using 1¾" screws, attach three angle irons to wall over right hand window, 1" from ceiling line, positioning them over wall studs at sides and at center (Diagram 9). Place "1 x 4" between top of angle irons and ceiling, centering it over window, and hold in place with ¾" screws through angle irons into underside of "1 x 4". Assemble other valance in same manner and hang at left-hand window (see photo).

TAILORED CORNICES
ON PAGES 48–49

MATERIALS NEEDED FOR EACH:

Two "1 x 6" x 12" for A
One "1 x 6" x required width less 1½" for B
¼" plywood, 12" x required width for C
Quilted fabric
¾" cording
Four ½" flat head wood screws
1" wire brads
Tacks or staples
Wood glue
Three 3" angle irons with screws

Glue and screw A to each end of B. Glue and nail C to A and B (Diagram 1).

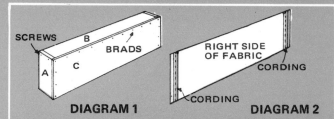

DIAGRAM 1

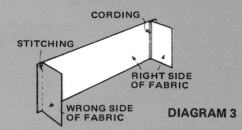

DIAGRAM 2

Cut one piece of fabric 14" x width of C plus 4" and two pieces of fabric 9" x 14" so fabric pattern will match when 14" edges are joined. Cut 3"-wide bias strips and cover cording. On right side of fabric, stitch a strip of cording down each side of piece to cover front of cornice so it will be along each front corner (Diag. 2).

DIAGRAM 3

With 14" edges together, stitch one 9" x 14" piece of fabric to each end of piece to cover front of cornice, following stitching line of cording (Diagram 3). Trim away excess quilting beyond seamline; finger-press seam allowances of fabric and cording open.

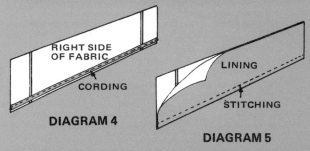

DIAGRAM 4   **DIAGRAM 5**

On right side of fabric, stitch cording along entire lower edge of piece to cover cornice (Diagram 4).

Cut lining fabric 14" x same length as outer fabric. With right sides together, stitch lining to outer fabric along stitching line of cording (Diagram 5). Trim away excess quilting and finger-press seam allowances open.

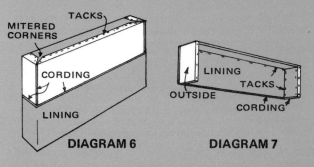

DIAGRAM 6   **DIAGRAM 7**

Allowing lining to hang below cornice, place outer fabric on cornice with cording along front corners and lower edge. Tack or staple outer fabric to top of cornice and along back edges, mitering corners (Diagram 6).

Pull lining to inside of cornice and staple or tack to sides along front corners, pleating in any extra fullness. Turn under raw edges and tack along top and back edges (Diagram 7).

Tack cording around top of cornice along front and side edges. Cover top of cornice with lining fabric, turning raw edge under along all four sides and tacking it over seam allowances of cording.

Locate studs in wall and attach angle irons so cornice will be at desired height. Place cornice on angle irons and screw in position.

RUFFLED BED CANOPY
ON PAGE 51
MATERIALS NEEDED:
> 55"-wide fabric
> 55"-wide lining fabric
> Snap tape
> Upholsterers' tacks

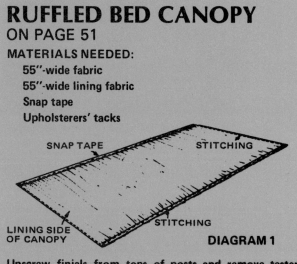

DIAGRAM 1

Unscrew finials from tops of posts and remove tester frame. Measure length of tester frame along top edge of one curved side. Using full width of fabric, cut a piece 1¾ times this length. Cut piece of lining fabric to same size. Cut two strips of snap tape 1" longer than length of frame and two 3"-wide strips of lining fabric the same length as tape.

Turn ½" to wrong side along both ends of fabric and lining and press. Place fabric on lining, wrong sides together, with both folded ends and selvedges along both sides flush. Stitch across each end ¼" from folded edges. Stitch two rows of machine gathering stitches along each side, placing them ¼" and ⅜" from edges. Make a mark every 12" along each strip of snap tape and every 20" along each side edge of canopy on lining side. Gather fabric and lining so marks on lining match marks on tape. Fold ½" under at each end of tape and place tape on lining, flush with edge of lining and leaving ½" of lining without tape at each end. Stitch along inside edge of tape *only* (Diagram 1).

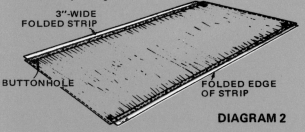

DIAGRAM 2

Fold the two 3"-wide lining strips in half lengthwise; turn ½" under at each end and press. Insert raw edges of lining strip between tape and lining, then stitch along outside edge of tape through all thicknesses. Place canopy on top of frame and mark position of finial hole at each corner. Make a buttonhole in each corner at these positions (Diagram 2).

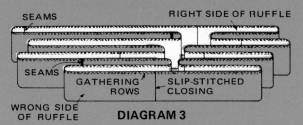

SEAMS

RIGHT SIDE OF RUFFLE

SEAMS

WRONG SIDE OF RUFFLE

GATHERING ROWS

SLIP-STITCHED CLOSING

DIAGRAM 3

Measure around entire outside edge of canopy and multiply by two for length of ruffle. Cut 9¾"-wide strips of fabric so pattern will match when seamed together across short ends. Seam strips together until length of piece equals above measurement. Cut and seam lining pieces together to same size. Place lining on fabric with right sides together and all edges even. Stitch along one long side ½" in from edge, and along the other long side ¼" in from edge. Turn right side out and press so a seam is along each edge. Turn under raw edges on one end and slip-stitch over raw edges of other end to form a circular piece. Run two rows of machine gathering stitches along edge with ¼" seam, placing them ¼" and ⅜" from edge (Diagram 3).

Mark every 12" along edges of canopy and every 24" along gathering line of ruffle. Place ruffle on right side of canopy with gathering line ½" in from edge of canopy along ends and along folded strip of lining, close to edge of snap tape; pin in place. Pull up gathers so marks match, then stitch ruffle to canopy along pinned line. (Stitching ruffle to folded strip of lining fabric, instead of directly to top section, eliminates excessive bulkiness and makes ruffle fall gracefully.) Using upholsterers' tacks, attach other side of snap tape to tester frame, along top of curved edges. Place canopy on frame and replace finials on tops of posts.

DUST RUFFLE ON PAGE 51

MATERIALS NEEDED:
    Fabric
    Muslin
    ½"-wide twill tape

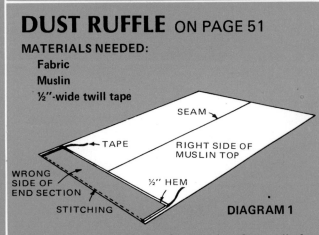

SEAM

TAPE

RIGHT SIDE OF MUSLIN TOP

WRONG SIDE OF END SECTION

½" HEM

STITCHING

DIAGRAM 1

Measure width and length of box spring. Cut muslin for top section of dust ruffle 1" wider and 1" longer than these measurements, seaming at center if muslin is not wide enough.

Cut muslin for two end sections 1" longer than width of box spring and 1" wider than depth of box spring. Cut

muslin for two side sections 1" longer than length of spring and same width as end sections. Make a ½" hem along three sides of each piece, leaving one long side unhemmed. Stitch a 10" strip of twill tape to each finished corner, and a 20" strip, folded in half, at the center of each side section if the bed has center legs. Place one end section across head of top section, right sides together and raw edges flush, with top section extending ½" at each side. Stitch together ½" from raw edges (Diagram 1).

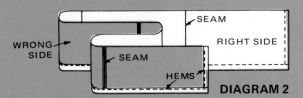

WRONG SIDE

SEAM

SEAM

RIGHT SIDE

HEMS

DIAGRAM 2

To determine depth of ruffle, measure from top of box spring to floor. Cut pieces for ruffle 4" deeper than this measurement across full width of outer fabric. Seam pieces together, matching pattern of fabric, until you have one strip 2½ times width of box spring plus 4" (for end ruffle) and two strips 2½ times length of box spring plus 4" (for side ruffles). Make a 2" hem down each short end; turn bottom edge under ½" and then make a 3½" hem (Diagram 2).

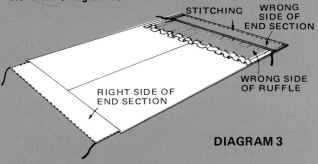

STITCHING

WRONG SIDE OF END SECTION

RIGHT SIDE OF END SECTION

WRONG SIDE OF RUFFLE

DIAGRAM 3

Stitch two rows of machine gathering stitches along top edge of each ruffling strip, placing them ¼" and ½" in from edge of fabric. Make a mark every 12" along top edge of muslin end and side sections, and every 27" along top edge of each ruffling strip. Pull up gathering threads of end ruffle until marks match those on muslin end section.

Place right side of muslin end section against wrong side of ruffle, with marks matching and top edges flush; pin together. Place ruffle on top section, right sides together, and stitch ½" from edge through all three pieces (Diagram 3).

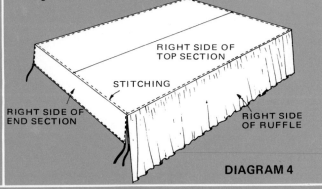

RIGHT SIDE OF TOP SECTION

STITCHING

RIGHT SIDE OF END SECTION

RIGHT SIDE OF RUFFLE

DIAGRAM 4

Gather side ruffles and attach to top section in same manner, with side ruffles meeting end ruffle at corners. Turn ruffles and muslin drops down and smooth seam allowances to underside of top section. Edge stitch through top and seam allowances around all four sides (Diagram 4).

Place dust ruffle on box spring and tie tapes attached to muslin side and end sections together around legs of bed. Tie tapes around center legs on either side.

COVERLET ON PAGE 51

MATERIALS NEEDED:
Fabric
Lining fabric
Cording, to be covered

DIAGRAM 1

Measure width and length of bed with sheets and blankets in place. Cut top section 1" wider and 2" longer than these measurements. If necessary to seam top section to obtain width, make it in three sections, using full width for center panel (on a double bed) with narrow side panels of matching width. Cut lining fabric the same size. Cut 1½"-wide bias strips of fabric and seam together as shown in Diagram 1.

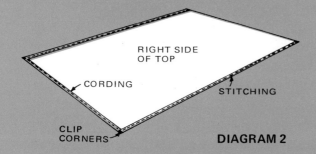

DIAGRAM 2

Cover cording with bias strips and trim seam allowances ½" beyond stitching line. Place top section on bed and place cording around three sides with raw edges of seam allowances flush. Clip seam allowances at corners and stitch in place (Diagram 2).

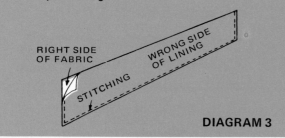

DIAGRAM 3

To determine depth of end and side drops, measure from top of bed to 4" below top of dust ruffle and add 1". Cut strips of fabric to this depth across full width of fabric. Seam short ends together, matching pattern of fabric, until you have one piece 1" longer than width of bed and two pieces 1" longer than length of bed. Cut and seam lining pieces to same size. Place each lining piece on matching drop, right sides together, and stitch around three sides (Diagram 3). Turn right side out and press.

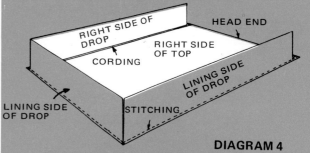

DIAGRAM 4

Place side and end drops over top section, with right sides together and raw edges flush; make sure drops meet at corners at foot of bed. Stitch drops to top section, following stitching line of cording (Diagram 4).

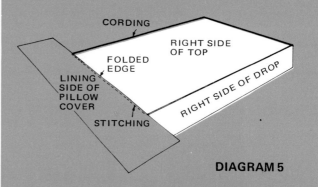

DIAGRAM 5

Turn side and end drops over top section, smoothing them flat. Place lining for top section over them and baste around three sides, following stitching line of cording and leaving head end open. Turn right side out and check to be sure coverlet lies smoothly. Turn back to wrong side and stitch drops in place.

Place coverlet on bed and place pillows in position at head end. Measure over pillows from back to front and allow for tuck-in under pillows; measure across top of pillows from side to side, from bottom edge of side drop on one side to bottom edge of side drop on the other side. Cut fabric and lining 1" wider and 1" longer than these measurements, seaming to match top section of coverlet (if top section is seamed) and to make fabric pattern on pillow cover match pattern on top of coverlet. Place lining on right side of fabric and stitch around all four sides, leaving an opening on one long side equal to width of top section. Turn right side out and press. Turn under edges of fabric and lining across the opening. Insert end of top section into opening, with lining side of pillow cover on top. Stitch fabric and lining to top across opening (Diagram 5).

America's Neo-Classic Era combined
classic forms and patriotic motifs

The nationalism that swept America after the Revolution was evident in an abundance of patriotic and classical motifs—a rather curious combination, since the classic forms were imported via France and England. The leaders and architects of the new nation (notably Thomas Jefferson) believed the ideals of the young republic should be expressed in the architectural forms of democratic Greece and republican Rome. Thus the important federal buildings of the period were designed in classical style, and classic details such as the acanthus leaf and the lyre came into fashion. At the same time (and inspired by the same sense of pride), nationalistic symbols such as the patriotic eagle and the thunderbolt were used for every kind of decoration. The foyer and living room glimpsed here capture the essence of this era in the classic window treatment (reminiscent of Greek toga drapery), the refined proportions of the wood-framed furniture, and the typical tier of portraits. Sofas, couches and settees were something of a luxury in the early Federal period; Sheraton noted their appropriateness in the well-appointed anti-room, "a place of repose before the general intercourse to be effected in the whole company." The couch in the "anti-room" opposite is covered in an eagle-medallioned fabric—a decorative use of the motif that expressed America's new feeling of nationalism and was used in every conceivable context. Directions for making the graceful swag and cascade drapery begin on Page 72 following this section.

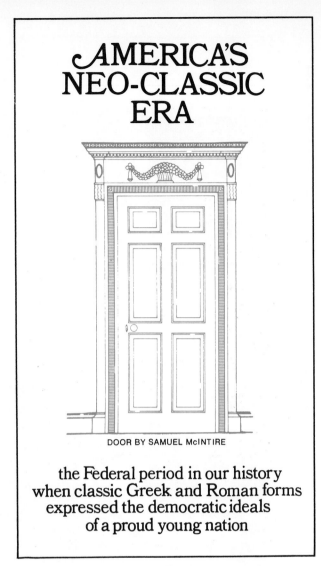

AMERICA'S NEO-CLASSIC ERA

DOOR BY SAMUEL McINTIRE

the Federal period in our history when classic Greek and Roman forms expressed the democratic ideals of a proud young nation

Attempting to pigeonhole period styles in terms of definite dates and specific forms is always hazardous, because the decorative arts flow from one era into the next in a continual process of evolution rather than of sudden change. But the American Revolution, with its vast effect on the political, social and economic conditions of the time, also caused a definitive change in architecture and interior decoration.

The Revolution interrupted the development of both culture and craftsmanship in America, and only after the adoption of the Constitution could the former colonists again turn their attention to the arts and amenities of life. Thus a natural break in the evolution of design occurred, and the term "Colonial" is used to designate the styles which prevailed before and during the Revolution, while the term "Federal" is applied to styles which became popular after the Federal government was established in 1789.

WHAT WAS HAPPENING IN ARCHITECTURE

A growing distaste for all things English was an inevitable result of the Revolution, and the English-Georgian style of Colonial design lost much of its former glory. This downgrading of pre-Revolutionary forms was spearheaded by Thomas Jefferson, whose influence was a dominant factor in the cultural revolution that followed the war. It was during this period that professional architects and designers first appeared on the American scene, and Washington, Jefferson and the leaders of this group endorsed a classical style for federal buildings, feeling that the new republic should be represented by the architectural forms of democratic Greece and republican Rome.

Archaeological discoveries in the Greco-Roman cities of Herculaneum and Pompeii had intrigued the entire Western world shortly before the Revolution, and Jefferson returned from his sojourn as Ambassador to France in 1789 with his enthusiasm for classical forms re-fired by a first-hand view of ancient monuments and by acquaintance with leaders of the neo-classic movement in Europe. The capitol of Virginia at Richmond, which he designed shortly after his return, was inspired by an ancient Roman building in France and established the columned temple portico as the hallmark of official American architecture. Monticello, completed in 1809, had much the same effect on residential building. Other influential architects of the day, including Charles Bullfinch of Boston and Samuel McIntire of Salem, also favored the classical approach. And an architect named Thornton, who designed the Capitol in Washington, obviously admired Greek architecture and ornament. The Greek revival dominated architecture in the East until about 1830, and was the accepted style in the Middle West until after 1850.

THE INTERIOR SCENE

No dramatic changes in the plan or arrangement of rooms took place in Early Federal houses, although the classic influence was seen in the introduction of circular, octagonal and oval rooms, and a permanent partition between the front and back parlors on one side of the entrance hall was usually dispensed with. The former partition was reduced to a frame for folding or sliding doors, or eliminated entirely in favor of an arrangment of columns that served as the only separation.

There was also a tendency to make the stairway more important, separating it from the entrance hall. Larger houses often had an attractive circular or semi-circular staircase extending through two or three floors and lighted by a lantern or cupola in the roof.

Definite changes did take place in wall treatments and in decorative detail. The ubiquitous wood paneling of Colonial days was largely supplanted by plaster walls covered with paint, imported fabric or wallpaper. Scenic wallpapers were imported from China, England and France, but wallpaper did not come into general use until after 1800, when technical improvements made roll printing possible as well as comparatively inexpensive.

Where wood paneling still appeared, it was usually only on the fireplace wall, but a vestige of the dado panel often remained in the form of a chair rail decorating the plaster walls. Corinthian and Ionic columns were frequently included in the wall treatments, but the detailing of cornice and trim was now apt to be executed in plaster instead of wood except in the Northern states, where wooden fluting and reeding continued, attesting the influence of maritime carpenters.

Mantels of wood or marble embellished with classic detailing were still the major decorative feature of most living rooms. Small panels under the shelf were carved with classical figures, urns, medallions and swags, but above-mantel decoration was usually omitted; separate mirrors in gilded frames were used instead. Elaborate detailing also appeared on the trim of doors, windows and arches, and pediments often crowned the doorways. Ceilings were frequently ornamented with classic patterns in plaster relief. The colors used in Early Federal rooms were

pale and rather delicate. The woodwork was usually white or cream, contrasting only slightly with the softly-tinted walls. But by the second decade of the nineteenth century, the impact of the Empire style was felt in fashionable circles, and the heavier colors already in vogue in Europe replaced the lighter tones.

FEDERAL FURNITURE

Furniture of the Federal period can be subdivided into two general trends and four different styles. The Hepplewhite and Sheraton styles, both characterized by delicate proportions and a general refinement, are designated as Early Federal. The furniture made in America from about 1805 to 1815 is often called American Directoire (or Early Empire), and is exemplified by the work of Duncan Phyfe and other American cabinetmakers of the period. The so-called American Empire style followed immediately, continuing some of the Directory forms in furniture made between 1815 and 1830. The final phase of the Federal period, between 1830 and 1840, saw the grace and elegance of the earlier designs supplanted by the heavy, cumbersome Late Empire style.

In England, some years before the Revolution, two architects of Scottish birth who designed both the exteriors and interiors of buildings, introduced their own version of neo-classicism. The Adam brothers, Robert and James, had made their own excavations and were enthusiastic advocates of the classic tradition. Their use of relatively simple masses combined with exquisitely-scaled ornament found almost instant favor, replacing the more cumbersome forms of the early Georgian style. The Revolution interrupted the normal flow of design inspiration from England to America, and the Adam influence was more evident in interior architectural treatment than in furnishings on this side of the Atlantic. But their profound effect on furniture design was transmitted through the work of English cabinetmakers copied here after the war and was the basic inspiration of much neo-classic furniture in America.

When normal relations and commerce between the two countries were resumed after the Revolution, the Hepplewhite style was already the prevailing fashion in England and was adopted to some extent by American cabinetmakers. It was the transitional style between the curvilinear forms of Chippendale and the straight, rectangular lines of Sheraton. Hepplewhite was especially noted for his inventive chair backs, particularly the shield design which was copiously copied in America, but interpretations of his graceful style included many other types of furniture—upholstered settees, tester beds, sectional dining tables, card tables with hinged tops, sideboards and secretary cabinets among them.

The Hepplewhite style was fashionable in America until about 1800, and its reign was overlapped by that of the Sheraton style, which became increasingly popular after 1795. The two were similar in many ways, with the same emphasis on excellent proportion and delicate ornament. In fact, American cabinetmakers often combined elements from both styles in one piece of furniture, and the two are sometimes simply grouped together under the "Neo-Classic" label. But Thomas Sheraton used straight lines and rectangular shapes to the almost complete exclusion of curves, except for graceful center splats on chairs, which took the form of curved and flowing vases. Carving, inlay and veneering were used by both designers but Sheraton was the first to employ porcelain plaques for decoration. The lyre was one of his favorite motifs, and he used reeding and fluting freely. His extensive use of these last three forms was copied by many American cabinetmakers; indeed, every conceivable kind of furniture made in America from 1795 to 1820 followed the Sheraton style.

Duncan Phyfe, a Scot who came to America in 1784 and is generally considered the finest American cabinetmaker of the early nineteenth century, followed the Sheraton manner closely, especially between 1795 and 1818, when he produced his finest work. He was both prolific and successful, to an almost phenomenal degree, and at one time employed more than a hundred artisans to produce his graceful designs. The finest examples of his work were made in mahogany and satinwood, with extreme delicacy of line and detail. The Grecian curve in chair backs and legs, and the pedestal table with curved and flaring legs were his hallmarks, but he used the lyre form extensively for chair backs, and sometimes for table supports. He also used reeding and turning, and his carved ornament was executed with extraordinary craftsmanship. Decoration included tassels, swags and rosettes, vases, bowknots and thunderbolts.

One of Duncan Phyfe's greatest assets was his ability to follow the prevailing fashion, and his adaptations of Directory and Early Empire styles continued his success into the American Directoire era. In this later period he used maple, rosewood and black walnut as well as mahogany, and his carved detail followed Grecian forms. When the late French Empire style came into vogue around 1840, he again followed fashion for commercial reasons. The result was massive, clumsy pieces which he himself called "butcher furniture," and his outstanding career ended in personal disappointment.

Although Duncan Phyfe did   ginate a style of his own, he added grace   refinement to every form he copied. He had a remarkable talent for selecting the best work of his predecessors and improving upon it. His cabinet work was always of exquisite quality, and everything he touched (until his last unhappy efforts) displayed impeccable taste.

A close look at Duncan Phyfe's work during the years from 1805 to 1815 almost defines the American Directoire style; his chairs and settees were among its finest examples. The French Directory furniture had been previously copied by English cabinetmakers, notably Sheraton, and Sheraton's designs, in turn, were closely followed by Phyfe. The influx of French aristocrats after the French Revolution undoubtedly was also a factor in the adoption of Directory styles. The typical American Directoire chair emphasized horizontal lines, with a top rail that tended to become broader and sweep backwards; sometimes the top rail was concave.

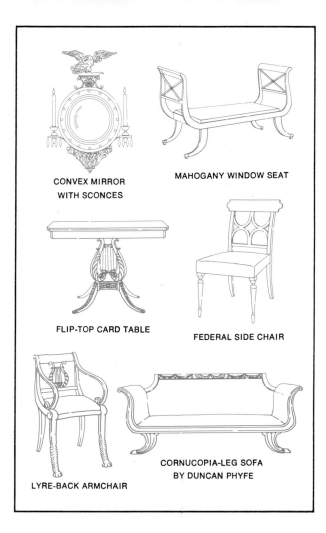

CONVEX MIRROR
WITH SCONCES

MAHOGANY WINDOW SEAT

FLIP-TOP CARD TABLE

FEDERAL SIDE CHAIR

LYRE-BACK ARMCHAIR

CORNUCOPIA-LEG SOFA
BY DUNCAN PHYFE

The American cabinetmakers were not inclined to follow the French Empire style of ornament, which was often inspired by Napoleon's campaigns and emphasized war-like motifs. The Americans preferred eagles, fruits, flowers, foliage and horns of plenty to express the abundance found in their own country.

Even as early as 1820, the heavier, more mechanical-looking forms of the Late Empire style began to be copied, and heavier moldings and less delicate carving were seen on furniture. Bold acanthus scrolls and leafage, along with the lion's paw and mask and other Empire motifs came into general use after that date. The impact of the later and heavier Empire style was felt more forcefully in the South than in New England, but no section of the country escaped its massive forms.

THE PATRIOTIC FERVOUR

America's new feeling of nationalism, fathered by the Revolution, found double-faceted expression. In addition to the classic forms deliberately chosen to express the nation's democratic ideals, patriotic symbols were flaunted at every opportunity. Before the adoption of the Constitution, the American eagle became the national emblem and soon spread its wings over doorways, clocks, mirrors, picture frames and tavern signs. It was used as a finial motif in architecture and as a support for chairs, tables and consoles. It became a pattern motif for china and glassware and was painted on windowpanes. It was used in every conceivable medium, and the round convex mirror surmounted by an American eagle became the most typical accessory. When the eagle was used in inlay work it was usually enclosed in an oval medallion and often held streamers in its mouth decorated with stars. Painted and inlaid stars were also favored in decoration, and were sometimes used to designate the number of states in the union when a piece was made. The thunderbolt was another patriotic symbol and historic scenes depicting important national events appeared on clocks and mirrors.

Derived from the Greek *klismos*, this chair had either saber legs or legs with concave curves. Typical sofas and settees were obviously inspired by the curvilinear Greek and Roman couches used by the ancients for combined dining and reclining. The ornamented front seat rail swept outward in graceful curves to form the side supports, and more curves appeared in the short cornucopia legs.

The American Directoire style was closely followed by American Empire, and some of the features of the former continued to be used in many chairs made in the Empire style. The dividing date-line between the two styles is a little fuzzy in any case, and the terminology is not explicit. "American Empire" is perhaps best applied to the furniture made in America between 1815 and 1830, with "Late Empire" being reserved for the years between 1830 and 1840, when the extraordinary grace and lightness of the earlier Federal forms were supplanted by massive and clumsy designs.

America's Neo-Classic Era

The outstanding furniture of the Federal period was produced by Duncan Phyfe

Duncan Phyfe was the most renowned cabinetmaker of the Federal period. His work followed the excellent proportions and delicacy of detail made popular by Sheraton, who was greatly influenced by French Directory furniture; Duncan Phyfe's finest work evolved from these two sources. The Grecian curve in chair backs and legs, and the pedestal support with concave, flaring legs were his two most typical forms. He was an extraordinary craftsman, and his carved ornamentation was exquisite. He used a great deal of reeding on chairs and sofas, and sometimes metal feet and ornaments. All these hallmarks are seen in the handsome adaptations above, gracing a dining room in the classic tradition.

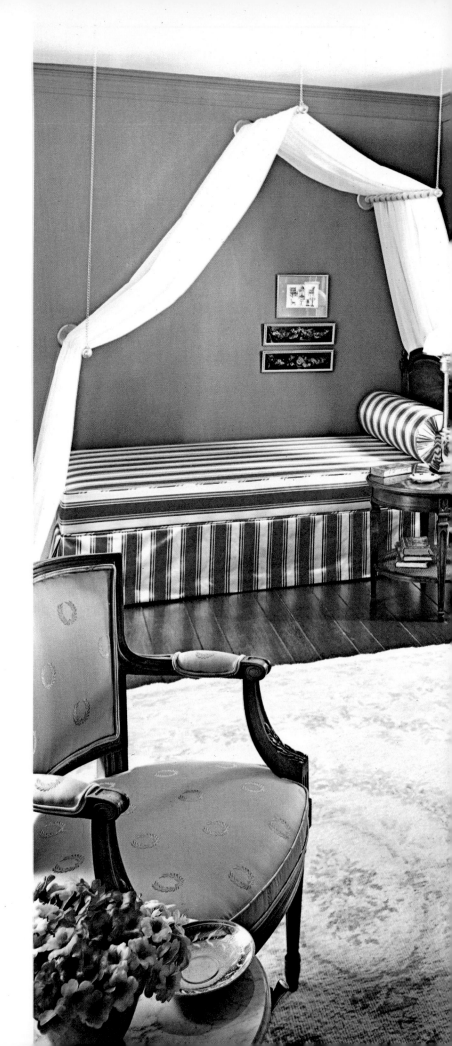

French-influenced Federal furniture has become known as "American Empire"

The years following the Revolution and the ratification of the Constitution saw a growing distaste for English traditions and English styles. This trend became more marked after the French Revolution, when migrating French aristocrats brought what furniture and household effects they could salvage with them, or had copies made by American cabinetmakers. Although the French mode never eclipsed the English influence, it was responsible for the term "American Empire" being applied to furniture made in America from 1815 to about 1830. And while the intricate French Empire style of ornament was not followed to any great extent, certain decorative features did become popular—among them the round wood columns used on sideboards and chests of drawers and the lion's-paw feet found on sofas and tables. The French influence is obvious in the bedroom seen here, although the chest with round wooden columns is actually a Biedermeier reproduction. The draped canopy above the bed was inspired by a Napoleonic campaign bed. The round bolster and drapery rods wound with striped ribbon have a definite French Empire look. You'll find directions for making these details on Page 73.

71

DIRECTIONS
FOR "NEO-CLASSIC" PROJECTS

SWAG AND CASCADES
ON PAGES 64 AND 65

MATERIALS NEEDED:

Muslin for pattern

Drapery fabric for swags and cascades

Lining fabric for cascades (Lining will show, so select it carefully to match or contrast. See photo.)

Twill tape

Staple gun and staples

FOR SWAG:

NOTE: The depth of the swag depends upon the height of the window; swags which are 15" to 17" deep at the center when finished are usually in good proportion. The width of the top of the swag is the same as the width of the cornice, but the piece of fabric for the swag is cut from 8" to 12" wider across the bottom, depending upon the finished depth desired.

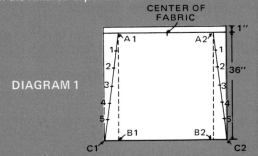

DIAGRAM 1

Place a piece of fabric 37" deep and as wide as needed right side up on a flat surface, and mark center of width at top edge. Draw a line 1" below top edge of fabric; on it indicate width of top of swag by marking points A1 and A2, centered on width of fabric. Mark corresponding points B1 and B2 on bottom edge of fabric. Decide how deep finished swag is to be. If finished depth of swag is to be 15", allow 4" from B1 to C1 and from B2 to C2; if finished depth is 16", allow 5"; if finished depth is 17", allow 6". Draw diagonal line from A1 to C1 and from A2 to C2. If you want 5 folds, divide the diagonal line into 6 equal parts; if you want 6 folds, divide it into 7 equal parts, etc. (Diagram 1).

Tack swag to cornice along 1" allowance at top edge of fabric. Fold at points 1 and pin to A on both sides. Fold at points 2 and pin to A and continue folding and pinning on both sides until all folds are pinned in place, smoothing folds from center out to sides as you work.

Cut off excess fabric on both sides in a straight line perpendicular to the floor. Place twill tape along top raw edge and staple it and the top edge of swag to top of cornice; staple through folds at either side into cornice, making certain staples will be hidden by cascades.

Leaving about 3½" beyond last fold, trim away excess fabric along curved bottom edge. Turn under a ½" hem.

FOR CASCADES:

NOTE: Cascades can be any length desired; the average finished length is approximately 30" at the outside edge. The inside edge is usually the same length as the finished depth of the swag. A cascade of average width is usually made with three deep side pleats.

Make a muslin pattern first, cutting it to shape shown in Diagram 2, with a diagonal line from bottom of inside edge to bottom of outside edge. Allow enough fabric (usually about 4") from outside edge for covering cornice return before starting pleats. Also allow about 1" along top edge for folding over cornice, and ½" on other three sides for seams.

Starting at long side where corner of cornice will fall, fold in three pleats; notch fabric to indicate folds and depths of pleats (Diagram 2).

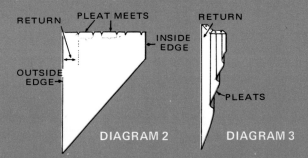

DIAGRAM 2   DIAGRAM 3

Use muslin pattern to cut cascades and lining pieces. With right sides together, seam fabric and lining together along sides and diagonal edge. Turn to right side and press. Pin top edges together and stitch ½" from edge; press. Fold and pin pleats in place; then stitch across top. Bind top edge with matching fabric or finish with tape to hold pleats in place. Make second cascade, reversing long side and direction of diagonal edge. Staple cascades to top of cornice (Diagram 3), overlapping ends of swags and covering staples.

BED CANOPY ON PAGE 70

MATERIALS NEEDED: (for 39"-wide bed)

Three 1⅜" diameter wooden poles, each 39" long

Three screw-on wooden finials

Three 6" wooden discs

Three lengths of gold chain: 18½", 24½" and 42½"

Gold paint

Three 1½" flat head wood screws

Six Molly bolts or toggle screws

Two lengths of 54"-wide sheer fabric, as required, to go from floor behind headboard, over 3 poles to floor at foot

Solid color fabric

Striped fabric or 1"-wide striped ribbon

Tacks

Staple gun and staples

1"-wire brads

NOTE: Ceiling in room shown is 8 feet high; tops of

poles are 12", 18" and 36" down from ceiling. Their positions, lengths of chains and length of sheer canopy will vary depending upon the height of your ceiling.

FOR POLES:

Measure circumference of pole; cut a strip of solid color fabric 1" wider than circumference of pole and 1" longer than length of pole. Turn ½" to wrong side along one long edge and, with fabric extending ½" beyond each end of pole, wrap fabric around pole, covering raw edge with folded edge. Staple in place close to folded edge. Fold excess ½" of fabric at each end flat against end of pole, pleating it to make it lie flat; staple in place.

FINIAL   SPIRALS   FOLDED EDGE

DIAGRAM 1   RIGHT SIDE OF SOLID COLOR FABRIC

For wrapping pole, use 1"-wide striped ribbon or cut a 2"-wide strip of striped fabric 64" long. If using ribbon, turn ½" to wrong side across each short edge; if using fabric, turn ½" to wrong side along all edges. Press folds flat. Starting at one end of fabric-covered pole, place one end of ribbon or strip of fabric on folded edge of fabric around pole and tack in place; wrap around pole in spiral fashion, keeping spirals evenly spaced and pulled smoothly in place. Tack to other end at folded edge of fabric (Diagram 1).

Paint finial with gold paint. Drill pilot hole in one end of pole and screw finial in place (see Diagram 1). Drill a pilot hole in other end of pole and in center of wooden disc for 1½" screws; drill another hole in the disc ½" from outer edge for Molly bolt or toggle screw. Paint disc with gold paint. Screw disc to pole with 1½" screw through pilot hole in center of disc. Attach disc to wall with Molly bolt or toggle screw through remaining pilot hole so top of pole is desired distance from ceiling and staples face toward ceiling. Nail other side of disc to wall with 1" wire brads. Make a 6½" loop in one end of chain and catch finial end of pole in this loop; attach other end of chain to ceiling with Molly bolt or toggle screw to hold pole in level position. Paint head of bolt or screw and touch up disc, if necessary.

FOR CANOPY:

Make a ½" hem across each 54" end of each piece of fabric. Drape fabric over poles as shown in photo and adjust folds on each pole so selvedge edges are hidden.

DRAPERY POLE ON PAGE 71

ON PAGE 71

MATERIALS NEEDED:

- One 1⅜"-diameter wooden pole in required length
- Two screw-on wooden finials
- Two wooden brackets
- Wooden drapery rings with 1¾" inside diameter
- Two 3⅛" diameter decorative brass holdbacks with 3⅜" posts
- Gold paint
- Tacks
- Solid-color fabric

- Striped fabric or 1"-wide striped ribbon
- Staple gun and staples

Cover pole in same manner as for preceding Bed Canopy, Diagram 1. Paint finials, brackets and rings with gold paint. Attach finial to one end of pole, put drapery rings on pole and attach finial to other end of pole. Attach brackets to wall at each side of opening, put pole in place and hang draperies from wooden rings. Hold conventional pinch-pleated draperies back with decorative brass holdbacks as shown in photo.

BOLSTER ON PAGE 70

ON PAGE 70

MATERIALS NEEDED:

- Round foam bolster, same width as bed
- Zipper, same length as bolster
- Two button molds, to be covered
- Cording, to be covered
- Nylon thread or buttonhole twist
- Fabric

Measure circumference of bolster. Cut fabric 1" wider than circumference and 1" longer than bolster. Fold under ½" of fabric along both long sides; place folded edges along center of zipper and stitch along both sides of zipper.

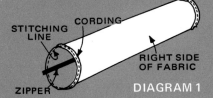

STITCHING LINE   CORDING   RIGHT SIDE OF FABRIC

ZIPPER   **DIAGRAM 1**

Cut 2"-wide bias strips of fabric and cover cording; trim to ½" beyond stitching line. Place cording around both ends of fabric, with raw edges of cording and fabric flush. Stitch, following stitching line of cording (Diag. 1).

Cut two strips for ends to length equal to circumference of bolster plus 1", and to width equal to one-half of diameter of bolster plus 1". Fold one strip in half, right sides together, with raw edges of short ends flush. Stitch ½" from edge (Diagram 2). Repeat for other end strip.

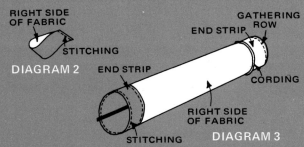

RIGHT SIDE OF FABRIC   STITCHING   GATHERING ROW   END STRIP

DIAGRAM 2   END STRIP   CORDING

RIGHT SIDE OF FABRIC

STITCHING   **DIAGRAM 3**

Place one strip around each end of bolster, right sides together and edges flush. Stitch, following stitching line of cording. Turn strips to right side. Using nylon thread or buttonhole twist, run a gathering row of stitching around loose end of each strip, ½" from edge. (Diag. 3). Cover buttons. Pull up gathering row as tightly as possible to form end. Sew button in center of each gathered end.

The Victorian Look

The pendulum of fashion swings . . . and some aspects of Victoriana return to favor. For aficionados of the opulent look prevalent during two thirds of the 19th Century, here is a typical ante-bellum parlor that could be reproduced today. Contrary to popular impression, the furniture of the Early Victorian era was comparatively conservative, without the excessively ornate carving so badly copied, a little later, from rococo Louis XV pieces. The window treatment here is also a moderate version of the fringe-laden swags, jabots and drapery that shrouded every window. (Even the fringe is swagged.) And the gilded metal cornice recalls the popularity of machine-pressed metal ornament. The heavy reds and deep greens are typical of Victorian color schemes and the extreme contrasts inspired by the discovery of aniline dyes. Only the chair in the foreground is an antique, and a chart for reproducing its authentic needlepoint cover can be found on **Page** 79. Directions for making the draperies follow.

The most obvious characteristic of Early Victorian furniture was rounded shape. The use of padding and upholstery increased as the rectangular frames of earlier styles became oval or semi-circular, with the arms and backs of sofas joined in a sweeping curve. The typical version of the 1840's was upholstered all over, but wooden framework was reintroduced a little later, and by 1860 often included elaborately carved panels as in the sofa seen above.

The Victorian Story

What is it that makes some aspects of Victorian decor so appealing today? Most Victorian furniture was without artistic merit; it was heavy, massive, and looked practically immovable. But that very quality of solid stability was much sought-after in Victorian life. Could we, perhaps, subconsciously be seeking a return to stability in our own lives by turning to styles and fads from an era when existence was more secure?

Or is it because the Victorians celebrated the curve, and after decades of being exposed to so many hard, straight lines, a certain amount of curves and curlicues now seems refreshing to our eyes?

One thing is certain: there is today a skyrocketing interest in all kinds of handcrafts, and Victoria's time was the golden age of needlework and all manner of allied crafts. Victoria herself as a young girl spent endless hours stitching, painting, cutting and pasting the elegant knicknacks that were known as "fancies." There must have been mountains of pincushions, ink wipers, needlebooks, purses and watch cases produced on both sides of the Atlantic as properly-reared young ladies in America as well as in England worked away assiduously on hand-made trifles with some pretension to usefulness, to be presented as gifts or offered at charity bazaars. The objects have changed, but many of the needlework techniques are back in fashion.

Victoria herself was born at the very beginning of the industrial age, and the utilization of steam and the advent of machine manufacturing was to have a profound effect on furniture design during her reign. In the years immediately preceding the establishment of an Early Victorian "style," four different influences were apparent: Grecian, Gothic, Louis XIV and Elizabethan. In architecture, the early Victorian years were marked by the dominance of the Gothic revival, and this trend continued during most of the Victorian age, resulting in a plethora of pointed wooden arches, vaults and windows as well as meretricious ornament and much stained glass. This strong Gothic influence, with its emphasis on carved ornamentation, spilled over into furniture design. After 1830, however, designers and craftsmen, in search of novelty, turned to many different sources for inspiration, and Greek, Turkish, Gothic, Renaissance, French Directoire, Empire and even Egyptian motifs were used indiscriminately, and often indiscriminately mixed. But the influence of the Louis XV style was apparently the most pervasive; unfortunately, it was interpreted with clumsy proportions and a fantastic amount of rococo ornamentation. Even cheap pressed metal decorations were gilded and applied to some furniture.

Because of this welter of conflicting influences, Victorian furniture cannot be considered a true or independent style; it was, rather, an overlapping mixture of styles, and because of the rapidly changing fashions and an insatiable craving for novelty, the period is difficult to define or follow. But contrary to popular impression, the Early Victorian furniture was comparatively conservative in the amount of ornament it employed and was also comparatively stable in style. The records and illustrations of the furniture displayed at the various exhibitions of the time, and particularly the catalog of the great Crystal Palace Exhibition in London, are misleading. Most of the furniture shown was chosen on the basis of novelty and inventiveness by manufacturers interested primarily in attracting attention. It is interesting to note that the illustrations in such catalogs were paid for by the exhibitors and are not a reliable indication of either the manufacturers' normal production or of the furniture in general use. The contrast is especially marked because the prime objective of Early Victorian furniture was comfort. Whether because of this emphasis on comfort or the invention of the coiled metal spring, padding and upholstery of all kinds became fashionable, and eventually all-upholstered furniture, without any visible framework, was developed. All kinds of cushioned seating arrangements appeared, including circular seats, the S-curved vis-a-vis, three-seated "confidantes," and derivatives of the Oriental ottoman, all elaborately corded, fringed, buttoned and tasseled in an orgy of decoration.

These changes in upholstery were significant; although only chairs, sofas, ottomans and such were directly affected, they influenced other types of furniture as well, and the resulting rounded shape, with all corners smoothed into curves, is the distinguishing characteristic of the Early Victorian style. At the same time, there was a tendency to join different parts of a piece of furniture into a unified whole. Arms and backs of sofas were merged in sweeping curves, and the fronts and sides of sideboards and chiffoniers were rounded into a semi-circular shape. Two major changes in chairs appeared. The first was the balloon-back dining and drawing room chair, with a rounded, balloon-shaped wooden frame which evolved from the horizontal yoke back and straight uprights of the classic style. The other was the entirely-upholstered chair with a high back, short legs and low, wide seat. The combination of these three elements gave a rather squatty-looking effect and illustrated the emphasis on comfort rather than style. In the 1850's wooden framework on chairs and sofas reappeared, and the single, double or triple curves of hump-backed sofas incorporated elaborately carved or open fretwork panels.

The use of Italian marble tops for tables (and also to some extent for sideboards and chiffoniers) was introduced in the 1840's, but there were few changes in the design of tables during the Early Victorian period, perhaps because they were often covered with an elaborate cloth that left only the lower part of the legs on view.

Sideboards, buffets and chiffoniers generally became semi-oval in shape instead of angular, and the more elaborate pieces were of heavily carved oak in the Elizabethan manner.

As Queen Victoria's reign progressed, there was a return to the rococo style in cabinetwork, with a profusion of curving lines and an over-abundance of fruit and flower carving. Rosewood, which was considered more fashionable than mahogany, became very popular for this type of furniture. In America, less expensive black walnut was often substituted for imported rosewood; this native product became more or less synonymous with American cabinetwork throughout the Victorian period.

No reference to the Victorian scene in America would be complete without mention of John Henry Belter, a cabinetmaker who opened a shop in New York City in 1844. He made some of the finest and most original furniture of the period, and was one of the first cabinetmakers to produce laminated pieces. Although some of his work was done in black walnut and stained oak, the best examples were in richly-grained rosewood, with thin layers of veneer glued together and then steamed and pressed in a special mold to obtain the mandatory curved surfaces. Each layer was laid at right angles to the next one before the molding took place. Then the surfaces were pierced with lacy, filigree-like designs and finally carved with fanciful flowers, foliage and fruit. More delicate and graceful than most Victorian furniture, Belter's designs were in great demand among well-to-do New Yorkers and the affluent of other cities during the 1840's and 1850's. But from about 1860 on, his work became less popular because the production of cheap, machine-made furniture increased, and jigsaw ornament was easy to make on the new steam-operated inventions. These machines were responsible for a vast surge of superfluous ornament, often on tawdry imitations of Second Empire pieces, that heaped disrepute on Victorian furniture.

Among a rapidly-changing succession of novelties admired by the fickle Victorians was lacquered, painted, gilded and be-jeweled papier-mache. Paper pulp was mixed with glue, chalk and sometimes sand, and then pressed, molded and baked into a consistency hard enough to be cut with a saw and take a high polish. A variation was made of strong sheets of paper pasted together instead of from paper pulp. Some furniture, including tables and chairs, was made completely of papier-mache, but much of the dazzling production was in smaller pieces and in accessories such as trays and boxes. Panels of papier-mache inserted into cabinets, screens and bookcases were very fashionable. Furniture made of bamboo, or made to look like bamboo, also became very popular. Because everything had to be decorated in some fashion, this was painted or gilded. Another novelty was wicker furniture, with the wicker woven and tortured into fantastic designs.

The inevitable reaction to ubiquitous Victorian curves and to tasteless ornamentation occurred in the late 1850's and 1860's, with a reversal to straight lines and revived interest in the Gothic style. Artists, architects and designers crusaded for a return to simplicity, sound workmanship and simple construction as opposed to the monstrosities of the industrial age. William Morris, an English architect, was the leader of this reform. His taste was emphatically Gothic; he admired the simplicity of massive oak furniture and inlay work made from fine woods. He also stressed the importance of hand work in decoration. His sound aesthetic principles influenced all the decorative arts, but were overwhelmed by the forces of industry and commercial expansion, and cheap interpretations of his ideas soon deteriorated into tastelessness.

The sound ideas of another well-known English architect, Charles Eastlake, also exerted a beneficial influence, but eventually met the same sad fate. His "Hints on Household Taste," first published in England in 1868, appeared in America in 1872. In it he minced no words about the deficiencies of Victorian houses and the decorative horrors inside them. He offered a whole new set of values, with the hope that well-designed furniture could be made by machine at prices the average householder could afford, and without being degraded by mass production. He suggested such revolutionary improvements as washable textiles that could be easily cared for, and straight, simple curtains on uncamouflaged rods instead of massive multiple draperies and dust-collecting cornices. His ideas and the sketches that illustrated them made many converts, who thereupon demanded "Eastlake furniture." Since such a style did not exist, furniture manufacturers concocted a style they referred to as *"after* Eastlake," and the architect's name soon became attached to a style which violated all the reforms he so earnestly advocated.

The Centennial Exhibition of 1876 had a remarkable influence on the last third of the Victorian era in America. It was the first such exhibition to be attended by vast numbers of the middle and lower classes, who returned home clutching their selections from the arts and crafts of fifty-one different countries. Japanese novelties were the decided favorites, and inspired the fascination with all things Oriental that lasted throughout the century. It was here that masses of Americans first saw bamboo and fell in love with it. Embroidered folding screens from Japan were another revelation, as were elaborate embroideries from Britain in rich screens, curtains and bedspreads. Exposure to Oriental art changed the Victorian's taste in floral decorations from hothouse and garden flowers to cat-tails, tall grasses and reedy plants such as the giant sunflower, hollyhocks and long-stemmed lilies. But the exhibits were far reaching, and the Japanese lacquered boxes, miniature pagodas and decorated fans carried home mingled with German cuckoo-clocks and beer steins, Spanish water jugs and Swiss hand crafts, all to be added to the clutter of bric-a-brac already decorating whatnot or mantel.

Another result of the Centennial was a re-awakened interest in American "antiques," and it wasn't long before spinning wheels and splint-bottomed chairs were hauled down from attics and dressed up with ribbons and "tidies" in typical Victorian fashion.

The heterogeneous styles and fads of the Victorian period reflected the taste level of the time—a time inexorably affected by the beginning of machine production. Although in disrepute for many years, they also expressed exuberance and a try-anything attitude that are typically American. Maybe that's why we find some of them attractive today!

Chart for Victorian needlepoint chair cover

ON PAGE 75

COLOR KEY:

⊡ CREAM	⊻ BLUE-GREEN	◤ DARK OLIVE
⊘ PALE GRAY-GREEN	◼ BLACK	▼ BROWN
⊞ MEDIUM GRAY-GREEN	⊡ MEDIUM YELLOW-GREEN	⊡ ORANGE
⊙ GRAY-GREEN	S GOLD	⊡ RUST
⊟ LIGHT BLUE-GREEN	Ⅲ LIGHT OLIVE	⊔ YELLOW
⊠ MEDIUM BLUE-GREEN	⊠ MEDIUM OLIVE	☐ RED

Turn to Page 91 for needlepoint directions

The Victorian Look revisited

Victorian taste ran to excess in all things, inspired by a mixture of many design influences, an insatiable thirst for novelty, and the advent of mass production. The Victorian ideal of richness was reflected in the use of color, and regal crimsons, purples and golds held sway for most of the period. Deep reds and greens were popular for upholstery and the multitudinous draperies that smothered every window. Here, the florid Victorian look features the same flamboyant red—but the upholstery is restrained, the window drapery simplified. A patchwork-printed fabric adds a lighthearted look, and the whole thing is given a crisp, contemporary touch by the bold black-and-white floor. If Victorian exuberance is your cup of tea, this is the way to have it today. Directions for the swag and cascade drapery follow.

Bentwood furniture has come to have a contemporary connotation, but Michael Thonet invented the process of steaming and then bending beechwood into flowing structural forms in 1840. He was also the first furniture designer to utilize mass production techniques, shipping his bentwood chairs unassembled. The three Thonet chairs above were produced between 1860 and 1876; bentwood chairs have been popular ever since.

ERNEST SILVA

The Victorian Look revisited

The popular taste level displayed during the Victorian era is generally considered lamentable (to put it mildly), but it's entirely possible to create a nostalgic setting replete with Victorian *flavor* without committing any of the decorating indiscretions so prevalent during the period. With color and pattern as your allies, the result can be as attractive as the charming "parlor" opposite. The pattern, of course, should be a floral—the more completely covered with flourishing blooms the better. Any form of floriculture, including bouquet-making and flower-painting, was considered a highly-desirable avocation, and the Victorians were as partial to roundness and plumpness in flowers as in the feminine form. So cabbage roses were among the most favored blossoms, and have a strongly Victorian connotation. Having selected a profusely-flowering fabric suitable for both drapery and upholstery, proceed to use it lavishly, and key your color scheme to it. (Notice that even a restrained Duncan Phyfe sofa acquires a Victorian flavor when covered in full-blown cabbage roses.) Add button-tufted side chairs covered in plushly glowing velvet, at least one marble-topped table (absolutely mandatory) and a few well-chosen accessories to complete the appealing picture.

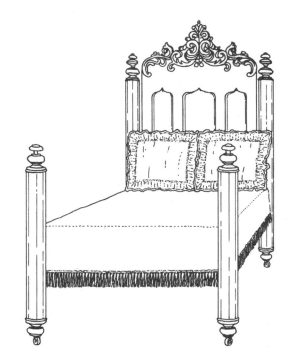

Massive beds were the rule during the Victorian period. Like most of the other cumbersome furniture, they were made of mahogany, rosewood or walnut and elaborately adorned with carving. Canopies and bed hangings were still favored in the early years, and the high, bulky headboards and ponderous posters that replaced them were almost as overwhelming. During the mid-Victorian phase, bedsteads of iron and brass began to displace those made of wood.

Victorian "Fancies"

inspire decorative beading for today's furnishings or fashions

"Fancy" they were indeed—the tiny purses, pincushions and needle cases that glittered with colorful beading. Even wall pockets for combs became minor works of art as industrious Victorian ladies plied their needles to make elegant knicknacks for gifts and charity bazaars. Exact copies of the authentic Victorian "fancies" seen here would be hard to make, because some kinds of beads are no longer available. But the same effect can be achieved, and would enhance today's fashions as well as keepsakes. The directions on the opposite page are for the basic beading techniques shown in the process of being worked in the composite photograph far right, for you to combine or adapt as you please.

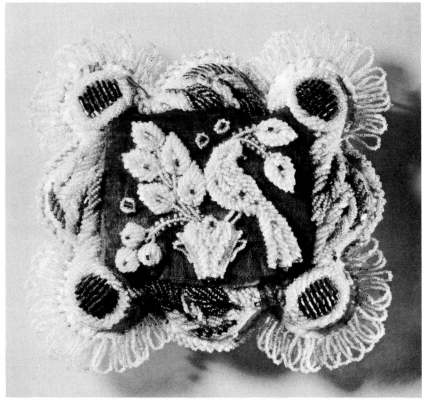

First, trace the design to be beaded onto thin paper, then cut it out and baste to fabric to serve as a guide for placement of beads. The beading is done over and through the paper.

The flat beading on the petals and leaf of the large flower at the top is done by stringing beads in rows so they will lie flat over an area. Raised center vein is made by stringing beads to fit from one end of a petal or leaf to the other, over the center of the flat rows.

To form tiny flowers next to large one, start with a bead at the center, then string seven beads and loop them around center one. Bring needle through first bead and fabric, then out on opposite side of center bead. To secure, make couching stitch over thread between beads.

For twisted stems, string a row of beads and anchor to fabric. String an equal number and weave them over and under the anchored row.

To form raised areas shown in petals of second large flower and in large leaf next to it, work beads in rows as for flat beading, stringing one or two more beads in each row than necessary to fill the area. This will force each row to arch upward, away from the fabric, when it is anchored. To complete flower, work high, raised rows around center and fill in with more rows.

For round flower, place a large bead at center. Work six slightly raised rows around the center, swirling them like a pinwheel; fill in with more raised, swirled rows. Around outside, make straight, raised rows very close together.

Fringes made of loops can be used to finish edges. String beads to make loop of desired length; attach end of loop to edge of fabric; repeat. Loops can be overlapped or intertwined.

Lattice edging shown below round flower is made row by row. For first row, string seven beads and catch in edge of fabric, forming a loop. Repeat along edge. For each succeeding row, bring needle through first four beads in first loop of previous row; then string seven beads and insert needle in center bead of next loop. Finish with wide loop across bottom edge.

Four single-loop edgings are shown below lattice. For first, string six beads, loop over edge of fabric from front to back; bring needle out above edge and repeat, forming overlapping loops. For second, string five beads and catch in edge of fabric. Bring needle down through last bead in previous loop and repeat to form flat loops. For third, string desired number of beads and catch on front edge of fabric. For fourth, string about five beads and loop around edge of fabric from front to back. Place loops close together to completely cover edge.

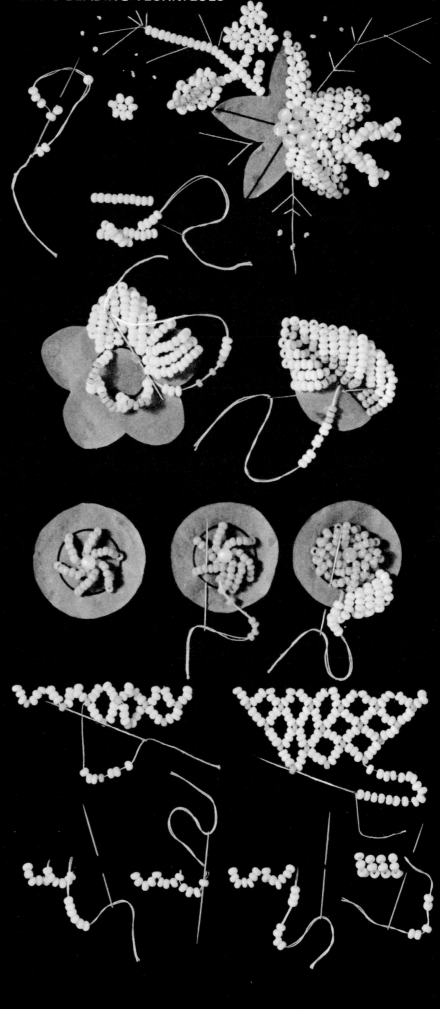

The Victorian "Cozy Corner" revisited

Every fashionable home of the late Victorian era included some version of a Turkish "cozy corner," preferably piled high with elaborate pillows and draped with rich Oriental fabrics. Doomed to become dust traps, they soon disappeared, but the idea of a separate, exotic-looking corner or alcove for "getting away from it all" still has romantic appeal.

A simple but effective "cozy corner" can be put together with little effort. Two studio couches are butted together in a corner, with box springs sitting right on the floor — or on a recessed platform, if you prefer. Make tailored covers and panel the wall behind the divans with the same print. Pile on lots of bright pillows in colors taken from the fabric and loop a heavy, tasseled gold cord along the wall.

This "cozy corner" would be a colorful oasis in an otherwise all-white or neutral room. Place a king-size mattress and box spring in the corner and paper the wall behind them with the most wildly-blooming wall-covering you can find. Place a simple 4" x 4" column on either side to set off the area. Slipcover the super-size divan in one of the colors in the paper (the background color if it's a bright one) and paint the posts to match. Line up a triple parade of puffy pillows in three more colors from the paper.

This "cozy corner" is really cozy—with an amusing implication of privacy. Start with a porch column (available at lumber yards) and place it opposite the corner so that brass rods suspended between it and the walls form a square. Two more brass rods go along the walls, and inexpensive Indian cotton panels (the kind sold for bedspreads) are hung from all four. Two wooden benches butted together are topped with foam cushions and pillows covered in more of the Indian print.

DIRECTIONS

FOR "VICTORIAN" PROJECTS

WINDOW TREATMENT
ON PAGE 75

MATERIALS NEEDED:
(for each window with 36"-wide opening and 44"-wide
   frame)
   "1 x 6" pine x 84" for E and F
   Six 1½" flat head wood screws
   Four 2" finishing nails
   Two 3" angle irons with four ¾" and four 1¾"
      flat head wood screws
   Sixty inches 4½" embossed-metal molding
   3½ yards 44"-wide velveteen for swags, cascades,
      facings and tiebacks
   6¼ yards swagged fringe for swags, cascades
      and tiebacks
   6¼ yards swag-and-tassel fringe for swags, cascades
      and tiebacks
   1½ yards gold cord and one gold tassel for each
      complete swag
   One large tassel for each cascade
   1" brass nails with round heads
   Four ⅜" brass rings and two cup hooks for tiebacks
   8½ yards 44"-wide velveteen for draperies (finished
      length 84")
   8 yards swagged fringe for draperies
   8 yards swag-and-tassel fringe for draperies
   Staple gun and staples
   Brown paper

FOR SWAGS, CASCADES AND CORNICE:

Make paper patterns for swag A, cascade B, facing C and tieback D in following manner: For swag A, mark a 28" x 25" piece of brown paper with 1" squares, mark center line connecting two 28" sides and enlarge outline from Diagram 1 onto one half of paper; fold paper in half along center line and cut through double thickness to form complete pattern. Draw pattern for cascade B to size and shape shown in Diagram 2, including cutting line for facing C. Draw 6" x 26" rectangle for pattern for tieback D.

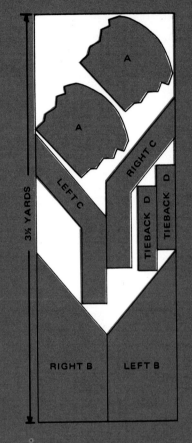

DIAGRAM 3

Velveteen is a napped fabric so cascades B should be cut with nap running from top to bottom. Swags A must be cut on the bias to make them drape properly. Cut two each of A, B, C and D from 3½ yards of fabric as shown in Diagram 3. When pressing, press on wrong side of velveteen with right side on Turkish towel or needle board.

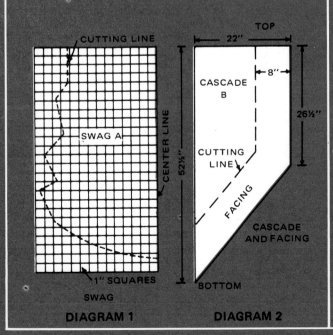

DIAGRAM 1   **DIAGRAM 2**

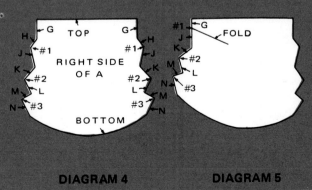

DIAGRAM 4   **DIAGRAM 5**

Diagram 4 shows swag A with folding points 1, 2 and 3 and edges G through N. Overcast bottom edge to prevent fraying. On left side, fold at 1 to bring edges H and J up flush with edge G; pin in place (Diagram 5).

Fold at 2 to bring edges K and L up flush with edge J; pin in place (Diagram 6).

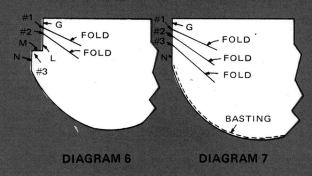

DIAGRAM 6   **DIAGRAM 7**

Fold at 3 to bring edges M and N up flush with edge L; pin in place. Turn ½" to wrong side along bottom edge and baste in place (Diagram 7).

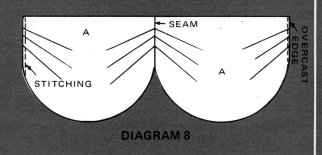

DIAGRAM 8

Fold along right edge of A in same manner. Fold, pin and baste a second A in same manner, and place two A with right sides together and all edges even. Seam together along one folded side only, ½" from raw edges. Stitch along other two edges to hold folds in place, and then overcast the raw edges (Diagram 8).

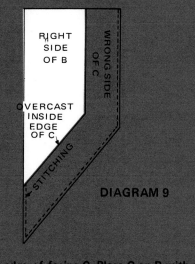

DIAGRAM 9

Overcast inside edge of facing C. Place C on B with right sides together and all edges even; stitch ½" from raw edges along two sides and up third side as far as overcast edge of C (Diagram 9).

Turn right side out so seams are along folded edges. Blind-stitch C to B along overcast edge. Turn ½" to wrong side along longest side and blind-stitch in place. Mark points W, X, Y and Z along top edge (Diagram 10).

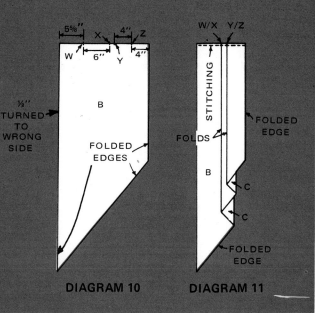

DIAGRAM 10   **DIAGRAM 11**

Form two pleats by folding X to W and Z to Y; stitch across ½" from top edge to hold pleats in place (Diagram 11). Make cascade for right side in same manner, reversing pleats at top.

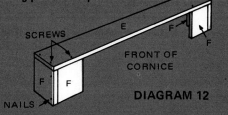

DIAGRAM 12

From "1 x 6", cut one E 48" long and four F 8" long for cornice. Bore six pilot holes in E, placing two ⅜" from each end and 1" in from long edges, and placing other two ⅜" from front edge and 4½" from each end. Nail two F together for each end, then attach E to F with screws through pilot holes (Diagram 12).

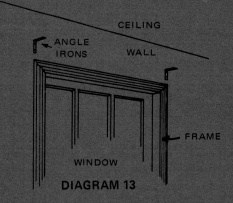

DIAGRAM 13

Using 1¾" screws, attach two angle irons to wall above window frame, one above each corner, so screws go into wall studs (Diagram 13). Place angle irons at correct height to allow swags and cascades to cover top of side drapery.

Stitch swagged fringe immediately above swag-and-tassel fringe along lower edge of swag so loops and tassels extend below edge of swag and stitching through fringes will hold ½" turnback in place when basting is removed. Stitch gold cord and tassel over seam in center of swag so tassel extends below edge of swag (see photo). Stitch fringes along inner and lower edges of each cascade and attach a large tassel at lowest point of each. Place swag on cornice so seam of swag is at center of E and top edge of swag is flush with top of E; staple in place across edge of E to hold top edge of swag in place, and to faces of F to hold sides of swag in place. Position a cascade at each side of swag so short side edge of cascade overlaps swag, long side edge of cascade is flush with back edge of side F, and top of cascade is flush with top of E. Staple in place. Using brass nails and a small nailset to prevent marring design, attach embossed-metal molding along edge of E, starting flush with back edge on one side, bending to go around corner, across front and to back edge at other side, piecing if necessary. Install drapery rod before positioning cornice (see Diagram 14). Place cornice on angle irons so it is centered above window; hold in place with ¾" screws through angle irons into underside of E (see photo).

FOR TIEBACKS:
Fold tieback D in half lengthwise with right sides together and stitch ½" from long edge. Turn right side out and fold so seam is along center of 2½" width. Overcast each end. Place fringes along center of right side and stitch in place. Sew a ⅜" brass ring to each end. Attach cup hooks to window frame just below cascades so brass rings on tieback can be caught on cup hooks.

FOR DRAPERIES:

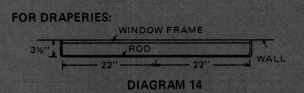

DIAGRAM 14

Finished width of draperies is based on a window with a 44"-wide frame and a drapery rod with a 3½" return (Diagram 14). Finished length of draperies is 84" from top to bottom. Nap on all panels of draperies should run from top to bottom when panels are seamed together.

Across full width of fabric, cut three pieces, each 98" long. Cut one of these pieces in half lengthwise. Taking a ½" seam, stitch a half-width to left side of one full width for right-hand drapery; stitch other half-width to right side of remaining full width for left-hand drapery. When pressing, press on wrong side of velveteen with right side on Turkish towel or needle board. Press seams open.

Make left-hand drapery in following manner: Along edge of half-width, turn ½" to wrong side, then turn 2" to wrong side for hem. Along edge of full width, turn ½" to wrong side, then turn 3" to wrong side for hem. Blind-stitch both side hems in place to within 14" of

bottom edge. Turn double 3½" heading to wrong side across top and blind-stitch down each edge of heading (Diagram 15).

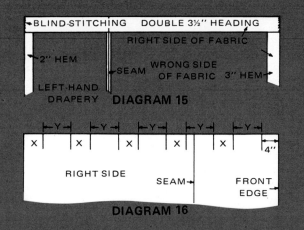

DIAGRAM 15

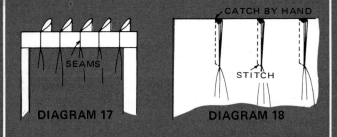

DIAGRAM 16

Allowing 4½" for spaces X and 6½" for pleats Y, make markings for pleats across top edge on right side of drapery (Diagram 16).

To form pleats, bring two Y together and stitch from top edge of drapery to bottom of 3½" heading (Diag.17).

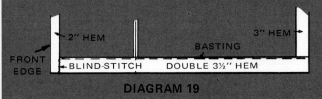

DIAGRAM 17　　　DIAGRAM 18

Fold each pleat into three equal smaller pleats and catch by hand at top edge. At bottom of each pleat, stitch from seam to front edge of pleat to hold three folds together (Diagram 18).

DIAGRAM 19

Turn up a double 3½" hem across bottom edge, with 2" hem at front edge folded over bottom hem and bottom folded over 3" side hem. Baste across top of hem. Finish blind-stitching 2" hem to bottom edge (Diagram 19).

Pin fringes along fold down front edge of drapery from top to 3½" from bottom edge, with tassels and loops extending beyond folded edge. Fold fringes at a right angle and continue pinning across width of drapery, 3½" from bottom edge. Stitch fringes in place, catching in hem when stitching across width of drapery.

Make right-hand drapery in same manner, reversing positions of 2" and 3" hems and reversing side of 4" space when marking for pleats along top edge.

NEEDLEPOINT DIRECTIONS
FOR CHAIR COVER ON PAGE 75
(CHART ON PAGE 79)

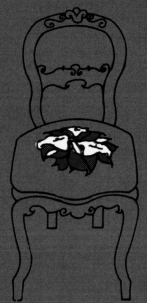

MATERIALS NEEDED:

Tapestry yarn in following colors and quantities:
- Cream, 2 skeins
- Pale gray-green, 3 skeins
- Medium gray-green, 2 skeins
- Gray-green, 1 skein
- Light blue-green, 1 skein
- Medium blue-green, 1 skein
- Blue-green, 3 skeins
- Black, 2 skeins
- Medium yellow-green, 2 skeins
- Gold, 1 skein
- Light olive, 1 skein
- Medium olive, 1 skein
- Dark olive, 1 skein
- Brown, 1 skein
- Orange, 1 skein
- Rust, 1 skein
- Yellow, 1 skein
- Red for background; amount depends upon size of chair seat
- Needlepoint canvas; 10 mesh-to-the-inch
- Tapestry needle
- Masking tape
- Muslin and paper for pattern
- Brown wrapping paper
- Rustproof thumb tacks
- Try square
- Soft wooden surface for blocking

To determine amount of canvas required, measure entire area of chair seat to be covered by needlepoint, including sides. Allow 2½" extra all around. To determine amount of yarn needed for background color, work a 1" square, noting amount of yarn used. (1¼ yards of tapestry yarn will work approximately 1 square inch of needlepoint.) Determine the number of square inches to be covered with needlepoint, then multiply by amount used to work the 1" square.

To make a muslin pattern, use a piece of muslin a little larger than chair seat. Mark vertical and horizontal lines to indicate center of muslin, and mark corresponding center lines on chair seat. Place muslin on chair seat, matching lines. Beginning at center and spacing pins 3" apart, pin muslin to chair seat along marked lines. Slash muslin to fit around back posts of chair and tuck it down between posts and seat. Pin corners to form miters, if necessary (Diagram 1).

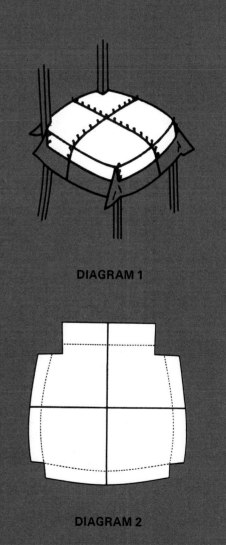

DIAGRAM 1

DIAGRAM 2

Mark all around lower edge of chair seat and around back posts, reaching down into tucked-in areas; mark on both sides of mitered corners. Mark lines around upper edge of chair seat to outline top of seat (design for needlepoint will be placed within these lines). Remove muslin from chair and pin onto a board, making certain threads are straight. Despite great care, the shape of the muslin will probably be slightly irregular; therefore, a perfectly symmetrical <u>paper</u> pattern should be made from the muslin version. As you make the paper pattern, check your measurements against the chair seat. Transfer horizontal and vertical lines and outline of top of seat from muslin to paper; cut out paper pattern (Diag. 2).

Mark horizontal and vertical lines on canvas as on muslin and paper. Place paper pattern on canvas, matching lines, and mark outline on canvas. Save paper pattern to use later as a blocking guide for completed piece.

Bind raw edges of canvas with masking tape to keep them from raveling. Use continental or diagonal stitch. (Diagonal stitch is preferred because it reinforces the canvas for pieces which will receive hard wear, such as chair seats.) Cut working strands of yarn 18" long, and use one strand in needle. In order to avoid skimpy-looking areas, keep yarn from twisting while stitching is being done. To begin, secure yarn by working over end on back; to end, go through stitches on back of work, and clip ends close to canvas. Be careful not to pull yarn too tightly; to keep yarn at proper tension, hold thumb on it until you have pulled it through canvas, lift thumb and pull yarn gently into place.

Using needle and black thread, baste along vertical and horizontal lines at center of canvas. Determine center of lily design on chart (Page 79). Following chart and color key, work <u>design</u> <u>area</u> <u>only</u> from center to right side (each square on chart represents one stitch). Complete design and fill in red background.

To block, cover a soft wooden surface with brown paper and tape paper pattern to board to serve as a guide. Place completed needlepoint right-side down over paper pattern. Stretch canvas to lines on paper and fasten with thumbtacks spaced ½" apart near edge of canvas. If necessary, straighten needlepoint area by pulling in place and then placing extra tacks near needlepoint. Wet thoroughly with a solution of 1 tablespoon of salt dissolved in 1 quart of cold water and let dry.

If the chair has a removable seat, take it off. Using vertical and horizontal lines marked on canvas of needlepoint piece as a guide, place needlepoint in position on seat. Use the unworked canvas for tacking to the bottom of seat. Begin by tacking center front and center back at edges, then tack center of sides, working toward corners. As you tack needlepoint in position, be careful not to pull it too tightly.

If fabric is attached to framework of chair seat, carefully remove the old upholstery fabric to see how it was attached, and use the same method for the needlepoint piece. Needlepoint differs from fabric in that only the unworked canvas should be turned back, to avoid bulkiness when mitering corners.

Because a piece of needlepoint is too valuable for the average amateur upholsterer to handle, it may be a good idea to have a professional upholsterer do the work for you.

CASCADES AND SWAGS
ON PAGE 80

MATERIALS NEEDED:
(for window up to 46½" wide)

"1 x 6" x 64" pine for A and B (ripped to 5¼" width)
One ¼" x 8" x 48" plywood for C
4½ yards 44"-wide fabric
2¼ yards 3½"-wide fringe
8 yards 1¼"-wide twill tape
Two 3" angle irons with two ¾" and two 1¾" flat head wood screws
Two decorative brass finials
1½" finishing nails
Four 2½" finishing nails
Wood glue
Staple gun and staples

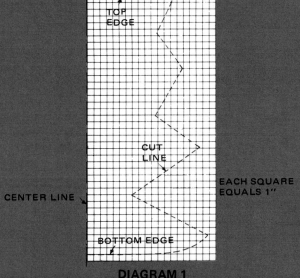

DIAGRAM 1

Enlarge graph in Diagram 1 to make paper pattern for swag. Cut 40" length across width of fabric. Fold fabric in half with selvedges together. Position center line of pattern (Diagram 1) flush with folded edge of fabric and cut swag.

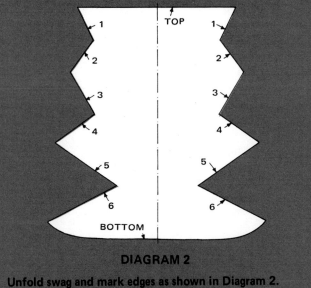

DIAGRAM 2

Unfold swag and mark edges as shown in Diagram 2.

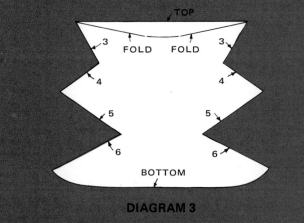

DIAGRAM 3

With right sides of fabric facing, bring left edge 2 up to left edge 1 and stitch ¼" from edge. Repeat with right edges 1 and 2 (Diagram 3).

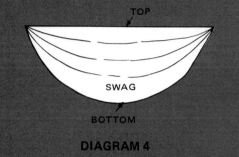

DIAGRAM 4

Continue in same manner, seaming edges 4 to 3 and edges 6 to 5 to form swag (Diagram 4).

Turn ¼" to right side along bottom edge of swag. Place top edge of fringe along folded edge, covering raw edge of fabric, and stitch in place.

Make second swag in same manner.

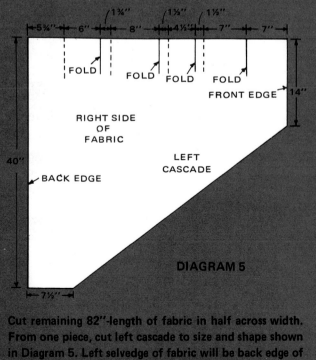

DIAGRAM 5

Cut remaining 82"-length of fabric in half across width. From one piece, cut left cascade to size and shape shown in Diagram 5. Left selvedge of fabric will be back edge of cascade. Mark positions of pleats across top edge.

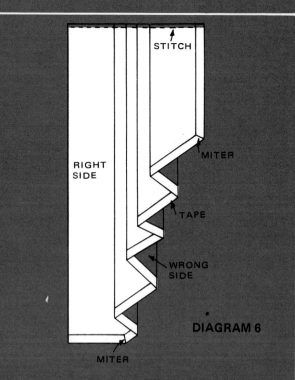

DIAGRAM 6

Place twill tape on right side of fabric along entire lower edge so bottom edge of tape extends ¼" beyond raw edge of fabric. Miter tape at the two corners; baste in place. Place tape on wrong side of fabric in same manner so bottom edges of tape are flush. Stitch through all thicknesses close to top and bottom edges of tape. Fold cascade along solid lines shown in Diagram 5 and bring folds to dotted lines to form pleats; stitch across top edge to hold pleats in place (Diagram 6).

Make right cascade from remaining 41"-length of fabric, reversing pattern so right selvedge of fabric will be back edge of cascade.

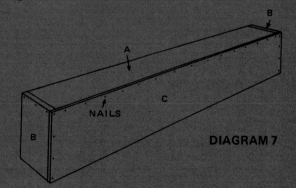

DIAGRAM 7

From "1 x 6" pine, cut one A to 46½" and two B to 8". Glue and nail B to each end of A with top edges flush. Glue and nail C to front of A and B so top, side and bottom edges are flush (Diagram 7).

Using 1¾" screws, attach two angle irons to wall above window frame at desired height, placing one above each corner so screws go into wall studs. Place cornice over angle irons and screw through angle irons into underside of A with ¾" screws. Place swags and cascades in position as shown in photograph and staple top edges to top of A. Drive two 2½" nails into each B at front edge so finials will fit snugly over nails at each upper front corner.

Turn-of-the-Century Nostalgia

Interior "design" at the turn of the century did not exist. There was no design at all to the heterogeneous scramble of furnishings most people had in their homes. The habit of mixing all manner of influences without regard for harmony or appropriateness was a hang-over from the Victorian era, when the popular taste level was deplorable. Pattern was piled on pattern, the walls were loaded with pictures, traffic patterns were completely ignored, peacock feathers and palms tangled with a plethora of bric-a-brac. In spite of it all, the period had a certain charm, which is looked back on with nostalgia by many people today. Here is how to retain the charm and the eclectic ambiance without the excesses. We've used only one printed fabric, manipulating the flower-laden stripes for the effect of pattern-on-pattern. The tufted, velvet-covered loveseat revives the overstuffed look in a delightful way and is contrasted with wicker pieces as popular today as at the turn of the century. The (then) passion for all things exotic is suggested by the elephant-head table and a *restrained* assemblage of antique accessories. Directions for making the big, fabric-covered ottoman follow.

Art Nouveau foyer of the Van Eetvelde house designed by Victor Horta in 1895. Foto Marburg.

The Turn-of-the-Century Story

The Victorian Era ended in a welter of confused and overlapping fads in interior design, with ideas imported from Italy, Spain, Germany, China, Japan, India and Turkey mixed indiscriminately with reproductions of the French Louis styles and American "antiques" which had been lately re-discovered and resurrected from attics. It was on this note that the 20th Century began, with a total lack of the consistency and harmony required to constitute a definitive "style." Well-meaning but ill-directed attempts to improve interior design by importing the arts of other countries were haphazard and illogical, and little effort was made to create an original or appropriate style for American homes. The extraordinary diversity of styles stemmed from a restless desire for novelty, and both historic and exotic themes were explored and re-explored in the attempt to find something new and different. The result was eclecticism carried to a ridiculous degree, with furniture styles jumbled together, pattern piled upon pattern, accessory crowding accessory. Traffic patterns within a room were completely ignored, and there was no semblance of what we would consider sensible or orderly furniture arrangement.

But even while 19th-Century tastelessness was rampant, there were indications that a change was coming, and that reform of interior design was inevitable. Reaction to the industrial revolution and the dominance of the machine inspired the so-called "Arts and Craft Movement" which erupted in England about 1860, advocating a return to simplicity and the honest craftsmanship of hand-made products. William Morris, the leader of the movement, insisted that art and design should be part of everyday life, inherent in even the most utilitarian objects.

Then in the 1890's a new development occurred, inspired by the same basic motives as the Arts and Crafts Movement. The phenomenon now generally known as *"Art Nouveau,"* or the new art style, spread through Europe and America with startling rapidity, sweeping across the boundary line between two centuries as well as two continents. Some art historians credit its beginning to Victor Horta in Brussels; others consider Chicago's Auditorium Building, designed by Louis Sullivan in 1888, its first manifestation. In any case, it was an almost simultaneous outbreak of individualism, a deliberate attempt to create a completely new style divorced from the past. The desire for novelty seen earlier in the Victorian Era was still a factor, reinforced by a wish to break with tradition.

The central and characteristic theme of the style was a sinuous, flowing line adapted from plant forms, primarily tendril-like but also reminiscent of waves or flames. Although it boasted of originality and an anti-historical basis, *Art Nouveau* was influenced, even if unconsciously, by Rococo, Gothic, Japanese and Celtic decorative forms— all intertwined in a surprisingly coherent style which only seemed non-derivative because the widely varying sources were difficult to identify.

The linear floral forms in iron were the hallmark of *Art Nouveau* interior decoration and were used on columns, railings, doorways, windows and wall divisions. The same swirly whiplash motifs appeared on floors and ceilings, giving many of the public rooms and private homes thus adorned a fantastic, fairytale quality.

Illustrations in the periodicals of the day and the ever-increasing indulgence in travel were largely responsible for the rapid spread of *Art Nouveau.* Rooms shown in the great international exhibitions of the era were viewed by thousands who would never have seen their like in private homes. Photographs of the same show-rooms were reproduced all over Europe and America, so their influence was enormous. The French architect Hector Guimard became famous for his graceful entrances to the Paris Metro, with their soaring metal flowers and ornamented railings in the *Art Nouveau* manner. Even the Eiffel Tower, one of the great engineering achievements of all time, is ornamented with *Art Nouveau* ironwork.

The craze for *Art Nouveau* also affected the design of furniture, fabrics, ceramics and stained glass, but it was basically a style of ornamentation rather than a true style in the sense that such a style is the expression of an era, apparent in its buildings, its decor, and its commonplace objects as well as its art forms. As decorative and diverting as it was, *Art Nouveau* was a style of art for art's sake, and the rage for it soon burned itself out. By 1905 it had begun to disappear, after becoming wildly extravagant in its insistence on originality. But as a protest movement it succeeded admirably, because it freed design from the domination of period styles and reliance on the past. The irony is that it became a period style itself.

Two interpretations of
The Turn-of-the-Century Look

Very much in fashion now: the nostalgic, cursive effusiveness of the early 1900's, which was a hang-over from the Victorian era. The restless desire for novelty resulted in the development of *Art Nouveau,* with its flowing, tendril-like forms. Revived with a tongue-in-cheek approach, and done with a light and knowing hand, its ornamental exuberance is a refreshing change from the recent plethora of hard-edged design. In the bedroom seen here, for instance, curves and pattern run rampant with a profusion of swirly flowers and foliage planted all over the walls, the bed, the window seat, the bench and even the lambrequin, whose meandering outline repeats the curves of the Art Nouveau clock. Using one wildly-flowering fabric everywhere in sight is an easy way to achieve a profusely-patterned look without completely overdoing it. (Notice that almost everything else is calm, collected white.) The lambrequin that creates such an interesting window niche is easy to construct; directions for building it are on Page 101.

98

A more restrained turn-of-the-century look recalls decorative
garden gazebos and Fourth-of-July band concerts, setting a
lighthearted mood for a combined kitchen and breakfast room.
Similar posts and balusters to create a porch-like illusion
can be found in lumber or demolition yards; the "gingerbread"
fans are antique-shop finds (try second-hand lumber yards, too).

DIRECTIONS

FOR "TURN-OF-THE-CENTURY" PROJECTS

ROUND OTTOMAN
ON PAGE 95

MATERIALS NEEDED:

Two 30"-diameter, ¾"-thick plywood circles for A, C
"2 x 2" x 100" for B
One 36" x 48" x ⅛"-thick Upsom board for D
3 yards fabric, at least 42"-wide
6½ yards 36"-wide, 1"-thick padding
One 1½"-diameter button, to be covered
½ yard ¼"-wide twill tape
Twelve 2" flat head wood screws
1" upholstery tacks
Staple gun and staples
String
Nylon thread

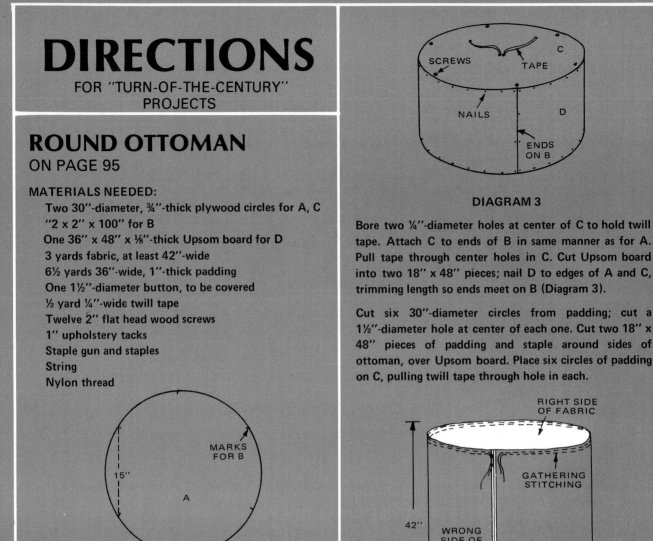

DIAGRAM 1

Make a string compass by tying a knot at one end, then tying a second knot 15" from first one. Place one knot on circumference of A and make a mark (also on circumference) at position of second knot; make five additional marks around circle (Diagram 1). Bore a hole for shank of screw at each mark, placing holes 1" in from edge of A.

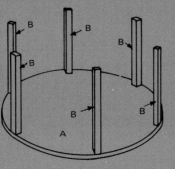

DIAGRAM 2

From "2 x 2", cut six B, each 16½" long. Attach one B to A at position of each hole so outside face of B is flush with edge of A; screw through A into end of B. Turn screws tightly so heads go slightly below surface of A (Diagram 2).

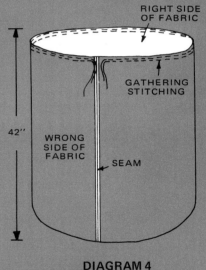

DIAGRAM 3

Bore two ¼"-diameter holes at center of C to hold twill tape. Attach C to ends of B in same manner as for A. Pull tape through center holes in C. Cut Upsom board into two 18" x 48" pieces; nail D to edges of A and C, trimming length so ends meet on B (Diagram 3).

Cut six 30"-diameter circles from padding; cut a 1½"-diameter hole at center of each one. Cut two 18" x 48" pieces of padding and staple around sides of ottoman, over Upsom board. Place six circles of padding on C, pulling twill tape through hole in each.

DIAGRAM 4

Trim fabric to 42" width and wrap around ottoman, wrong side out; pin fabric to mark seam. Remove fabric from ottoman and stitch seam, matching fabric pattern. Using nylon thread in bobbin, stitch two gathering rows ½" and ¼" from top edge of fabric. Press seam open (Diagram 4).

Cover button, and turn fabric tube right-side out. Pull up gathering threads, leaving just enough of an opening for tapes to pass through; secure gathering threads. Place fabric on ottoman and pull tapes through opening; put one tape through shank of button and tie tapes so button is secured and padding is depressed slightly at center (see photo).

Smooth fabric down over sides and onto bottom face of A, making sure fabric pattern is even around lower edge. Turn under raw edge of fabric; staple to bottom face of A.

BOLSTERS ON PAGES 98-99

See directions for covering bolster on Page 73. Use bolster same width as bench and substitute two tassels for covered buttons; sew one to center of each end.

LAMBREQUIN ON PAGE 98

MATERIALS NEEDED:

(for lambrequin 60" wide, 84" high)

Clear pine: one "1 x 16" x 60" for A
two "1 x 10" x 84" for B
one "1 x 4" x 60" for D
two "1 x 4" x 83¼" for E

One ¼" x 16" x 16" Masonite for C

Four 1½" flat head wood screws

Twelve ⅞" round head wood screws

Six 2½" angle irons with twelve ⅝" screws

Six hollow-wall fasteners

1½" finishing nails, ¾" wire brads

Wood glue

Wallpaper and paste

Decorative trim

Basecoat

Sizing

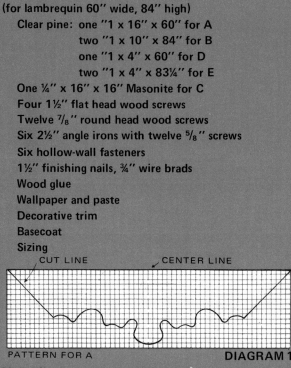

PATTERN FOR A   DIAGRAM 1

Mark 1" squares on "1 x 16" and draw scalloped outline for lower edge of A by enlarging pattern given in Diagram 1, making 45° angles at each end. Cut out A along outline.

PATTERN FOR B   DIAGRAM 2

Draw pattern and cut two B from "1 x 10" in same manner, following outline given in Diagram 2, making a 45° angle at top end.

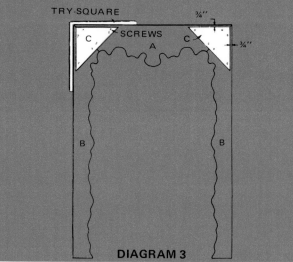

DIAGRAM 3

Mark a line ¾" in from top edge of A. Mark a line 18" long down outside edge from top of each B, ¾" in from edge. Cut the 16" Masonite square in half diagonally to form two triangles C.

Drill six pilot holes for ⅞" screws in each C in positions shown in Diagram 3. Place A and B together with 45° angles butting; place a C over joining of A and B at each top corner, with short sides of C along marked lines on A and B; check with try square and attach both C to A and B with ⅞" round head screws (Diagram 3).

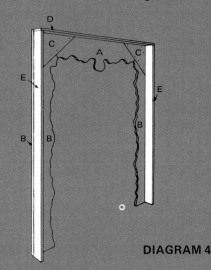

DIAGRAM 4

Drill two pilot holes for 1½" screws at each end of D, placing them ⅜" from ends and 1" in from each side edge. Glue and screw D to both E, keeping ends of D flush with outside faces of E. Glue and nail A and B to edges of D and E, keeping all outside edges flush (Diagram 4).

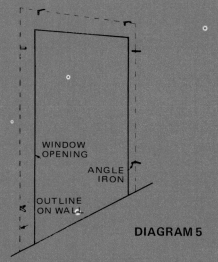

DIAGRAM 5

Hold lambrequin in position at window and mark inside edges of D and E on wall. Attach angle irons to wall with hollow-wall fasteners in positions shown (Diagram 5).

Countersink screws and nail heads. Fill all cracks and holes with wood filler. Sand all surfaces smooth. Apply basecoat, then sizing. Cover outside face and edges of lambrequin with wallpaper, clipping paper to fold around scalloped edges of A and B. Using ¾" brads, nail decorative trim around scalloped edges of A and B.

TRADITION BROUGHT-UP-TO-DATE;

The Past-and-Present Look _____

Having seen and studied (to some extent, at least) the major American styles of traditional decorating, you may still be undecided about the look you want to live with. Perhaps you've concluded that a definite period style is too conventional or too formal for your life style. That's true of many families, and there *is* an alternative—a popular decorating style that has been developing over a period of years and has now emerged with a definite personality. Its main characteristic is a mix of comfortable traditional furniture in a decidedly contemporary setting. The familiar furniture styles bring warmth and solidity to today's architecturally plain interiors. But the colors and patterns used are predominantly contemporary. (If a fabric pattern is traditional, the coloring is updated.) A clean, uncluttered look and a casual, informal air contribute to the contemporary ambiance.

Above all, there is a definite flair—even a touch of flamboyance—in bold touches of color or pattern, unexpected color alliances, or offbeat but pleasing combinations of the past and present. You might find originals of the handsome 18th-Century furniture opposite in a museum—and in a paneled room, at that. But here, the rough-sawn boards painted white and contrasted by blue moldings and cornice are a contemporary interpretation of the traditional setting. And while the fabric that covers the camel-back love-seat and Queen Anne style chairs is traditional in pattern, the blue-and-white color scheme updates it. Note that the important painting is decidedly contemporary. (Notice, too, that its vivid splashes of relieving color are repeated in bunches of flowers on the *unmatched* chests at either side.) You'll find directions for applying the molding on Page 112 following this section.

ERNEST SILVA

The Past-and-Present Look

gives Oriental elegance a contemporary ambiance

Never completely out of fashion, the Oriental look in furniture (and decorating in general) is now very much in favor – a happy circumstance for anyone who likes a sophisticated mixture of traditional and contemporary elements. As early as the middle of the 17th Century, New England sailing ships sailed to the Orient and back, returning with a cargo of artistic treasures from the East. And Thomas Chippendale, the famous 18th-Century cabinetmaker so widely copied in the Colonies, incorporated so many Chinese forms and figures, so much latticework and fretwork in many of his designs that his work in the Chinese manner came to be known as "Chinese Chippendale." So the Oriental influence has been a traditional factor in the decorative art of this country. The surprising thing is that it blends so beautifully with furnishings in a contemporary mood. Here, a gilded Japanese screen and a Chinoiserie cocktail table add a richly Oriental touch to a living room of quiet elegance. The chest and chairs are also traditional in feeling, but the sofa and the fabric that covers it are very much of today. A companion fabric in the same monochromatic color scheme of beige to taupe covers the walls and one of the armchairs, contrasting the rich brown rug and the warming touches of gold that serve as accents.

One decorating dilemma that faces many people – and especially young couples: how to introduce a family heirloom or a favorite reproduction into a setting that's predominantly contemporary. It takes taste and perhaps a touch of daring, but you can certainly do it – and have the "past" and "present" elements live happily together. The dining room at the left belongs to a couple who inherited four handsome Queen Anne chairs – and they love the classic curves of the cabriole legs and urn-shaped backs. But their table is steel and glass, their walls and floor stark white, and the painting they splurged on strictly abstract. How did they make it all work together? By letting the contemporary mood dominate and bridging the generation gap with pattern and color – in this case, a striking fabric with a vaguely Oriental pattern that complements both traditional curves and contemporary lines. Its vibrant coloring unites the dining area and the screens that form a niche to display the painting.

At the right, another room in which traditional furniture feels right at home in a non-traditional setting. Again, color and pattern play the mediator. The contemporary color scheme of brown, black and white is surrounded by silvery wallcovering, and a geometric pattern is used to cover both the Chippendale-style chair and the contemporary ottomans. The ceiling was painted the same brown as the rug, and the floor was striped with solid-color tiles for another touch of pattern.

ROBERT HOEBERMANN

ERNEST SILVA

The Past-and-Present Look

contrasts contemporary with a touch of tradition

A sentimental attachment to a treasured family heirloom (or almost any other traditional piece) doesn't have to be a handicap – even if everything else you own was designed after 1950 and your home is a masterpiece of modern architecture. The contrast between classic curves and spare, straight lines, between a reasonable amount of ornamentation and none at all adds interest and flavor to any room. The trick is to set off the unique element and make a point of its difference – especially if it's a really fine piece of furniture. The contrast will spotlight and enhance its good qualities. Here, a handsome Philadelphia highboy stands in solitary elegance against one wall, almost like an interesting piece of sculpture to be admired by anyone who enters the foyer. No attempt is made to disguise its chronological difference or make it merge into the contemporary mood of the room; it's simply a marvelous counterpoint to the other pieces of furniture, and its graceful curves and delicate carving seem all the more notable in contrast to the square-cut solidity of the contemporary pieces. Of course, a unity of coloring helps, and the warm wood tones of the highboy blend nicely with the tawny browns and rusts of the upholstered pieces and the area rug.

ROBERT HOEBERMANN

The Past-and-Present Look
can be an eclectic mixture of periods and styles

You may admire many styles of decorating without being addicted to any one period, and want to surround yourself with very personal choices in furniture and accessories. More power to you. The most interesting rooms in the world are expressions of personality and therefore have character and individuality. The bed-sitting room seen here was obviously put together by an independent thinker who prefers rather formal traditional furniture but has the wit and daring to add a flash of whimsy and then use a vibrant color scheme in a very contemporary manner. The hot oranges and forceful blues are laced with lots of white, and white outlines the off-beat "Regency" bed. The desk is line-for-line Chippendale, the lacquered armchair is a modern interpretation of a Chippendale classic, and the table is Victorian. In contrast, the shag carpeting is very contemporary, and the decorative Chinese garden seat used as a small table adds a final eclectic touch. Tying it all together: a printed fabric that's an updated version of a traditional crewel pattern.

REG VAN CUYLENBURG

111

DIRECTIONS
FOR "PAST-AND-PRESENT" PROJECTS

APPLYING MOLDINGS
ON PAGE 103

MATERIALS NEEDED:

Each of the following x perimeter of room:
    for ceiling: "1 x 2" common pine for A
               ¾" x 4¼" casing molding for B
               1⅜ " x 2¾" base molding for C
    for floor: ¾" x 4¾" casing molding for D
To outline "panels":
    ⁷⁄₁₆" x 1⅛ " panel molding: eleven 72" lengths
    and two 96" lengths for one 12'10" wide x 8'
    high wall as shown in photo and diagrams
2" finishing nails
1½" wire brads
Basecoat and paint

Placing 1" face against ceiling and 2" face against wall, nail A to wall at ceiling line around entire room (see Diagram 2). Use finishing nails and stagger them so they do not split A; it is not necessary to miter ends of A.

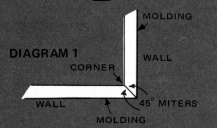

DIAGRAM 1

Cut 45° angles at ends of all molding pieces to be used at ceiling and floor so they will fit into corners of room and form smooth joints. Diagram 1 shows top view of

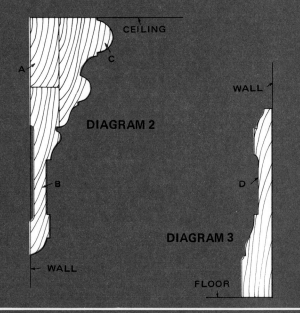

DIAGRAM 2

DIAGRAM 3

how angles must be cut for inside corners. Sand, then apply basecoat and paint, following manufacturer's directions. Using wire brads, attach B to wall directly under A, then attach C along ceiling line so it covers A and upper part of B; use a small nailset to drive brads slightly below surface and to prevent hammer marks. Touch up nail heads with paint. Diagram 2 shows cross-section of A, B and C in place.

Using brads, attach D at floor line around room in same manner. Diagram 3 shows cross-section of D in place.

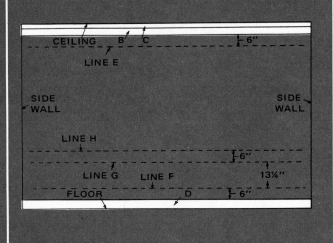

DIAGRAM 4

Mark wall to position moldings that outline non-existent "panels" in following manner: Use a soft pencil and mark lines lightly so they can be erased if not covered by molding. Use a level to mark all horizontal lines and a plumb bob to establish all vertical lines. Mark horizontal line E 6" down from bottom of B. Mark line F 6" up from top of D. Mark line G 13¼" above line F, then mark line H 6" above line G (Diagram 4).

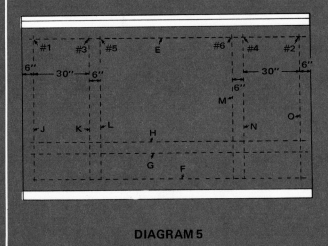

DIAGRAM 5

Mark six points on line E as follows: #1 and #2, 6" from side walls; #3 and #4, 30" from #1 and #2; #5 and #6, 6" from #3 and #4. Mark vertical lines J, K, L, M, N and O from these six points to line F (Diagram 5).

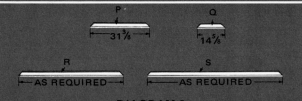

DIAGRAM 6

Cut molding to outline "panels" in the following lengths: Eight P, 31⅜" long; six Q, 14⅝" long; six R and four S in required lengths. Cut one Q and one R from each of six 72" lengths; cut two P from one 72" length; cut three P from each of two 96" lengths; cut one S from each of four 72" lengths. Cut a 45° angle at both ends of each piece (Diagram 6).

Sand and paint molding. Using brads and centering molding on marked lines, attach to wall in following order so 45° angles form square corners: P, S and P along line E; R along each long vertical line; P, S and P along line H.

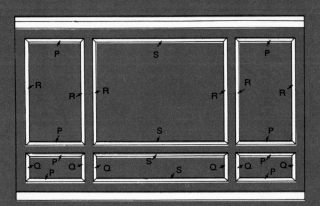

DIAGRAM 7

Attach lower P, S and Q in same order (Diagram 7). Erase pencil lines. Touch up nail heads with paint.

APPLYING CEILING MOLDINGS ON PAGE 107

MATERIALS NEEDED:
Enough of each of the following to go around
   entire perimeter of room:
      "1 x 4" common pine for A
      ¾" x 2¾" casing molding for B
      ¾" x 3¾" casing molding for C
      ½" x ¾" lattice strips for D
      ⁷⁄₁₆" x 1⅜" panel molding for E
   1" and 1½" wire brads
   2" finishing nails
   Basecoat, brown and white paint

Diagram 1 shows cross-section of all parts in place. Check moldings you are using against positions shown in Diagram 1 and make any adjustments necessary so bottom edges of C and E will overlap other parts in desired positions.

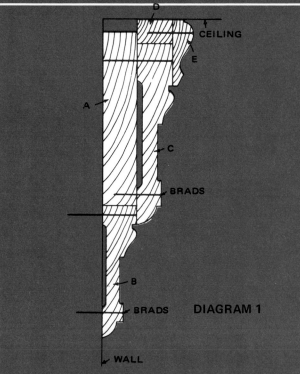

DIAGRAM 1

Measure down 3⅝" from ceiling and mark a line around entire room, checking with a level as you work. Placing 4" face against wall and bottom edge along marked line, nail A around room. Use finishing nails and stagger them so they do not split A; it is not necessary to miter ends of A at corners.

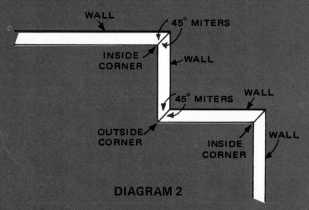

DIAGRAM 2

Cut 45° angles at ends of B where necessary so pieces will fit together at corners of room and form smooth joints. Diagram 2 shows top view of how angles must be cut for inside and outside corners. Sand and apply basecoat and white paint to all B parts, following manufacturer's directions.

Using 1½" brads through flat face of B at top, nail B to wall under A. Using 1" brads, nail through flat face of B at bottom; use a small nailset to drive heads of brads slightly below surface and to prevent hammer marks (see Diagram 1). Touch up nail heads with paint.

Using 1" brads, nail lattice D to ¾" top edge of molding C; cut 45° angles at ends, sand and paint brown. Attach C and D to A as before, overlapping top of B (see Diagram 1). Touch up nail heads at bottom. Cut 45° angles at ends of E; sand, paint white and attach with 1" brads (see Diagram 1). Touch up nail heads.

WINDOW TREATMENTS to complement traditional rooms

Windows are almost always an important feature of a room, and can add immeasurably to the mood or style you want to establish. But consider the *function* of the window treatment first. Do you want to frame the view or obscure it, admit maximum light or shade the room from glare? Only then go on to style and color.

A glowing golden room with versatile draperies that admit a moderate amount of light by day and can close out the rest of the world at night. The furniture is predominantly traditional in feeling, but no specific period style was followed. (The contemporary steel and glass bar provides an eclectic touch of contrast.) The mood of the room is warm and gracious, and the window treatment complements it perfectly. Directions for making the shirred-top draperies that form a self-valance follow.

The graceful swags and cascades that frame the windows below in the 18th-Century manner do much to establish the mood of the room – even though the loveseat they flank is more modern than traditional. (An 18th-Century print ties them together.) These two 36"-wide windows happen to be tall, but the same floor-to-ceiling treatment could be used for windows of any height. Directions for making the swags and cascades follow.

WINDOW TREATMENTS to complement traditional rooms

Adding color, warmth and richness to the living room above: a window treatment with a touch of Chinoiserie that blends with the traditional 18th-Century furniture and brightens the dark wood-paneled walls. Directions for making the scalloped cornice covered with printed chintz are on Page 123. The cornice shown is 48″ wide, but the pattern can easily be adjusted to fit a window up to 54″ wide.

Lined draperies that don't require a cornice have a classic traditional look and provide lots of opportunity for color and fabric coordination. In the country bedroom at the right, a flower-patterned toile covers the walls and wing chair, lines both book shelves and drapery, even makes the pleated dust ruffle for a completely unified look. Directions for making the draperies are on Page 124.

VAN NES

THE WELL-DRESSED BED
is the focal point of a traditional bedroom

Don't settle for a humdrum bed just because you want a traditional look. Colonial four-posters and the tent-like beds of the English Regency period offer unlimited inspiration for unusual and visually exciting treatments that will add color and character to any bedroom.

The imposing look of a draped and canopied four-poster can be adapted to suit a small room where the complete treatment might seem over-powering. The solution – a decorative valance and draperies contrast-ing a wall panel of pleated fabric above the head of the bed. Make a scalloped coverlet to match the valance, a dust ruffle to match the panel for the dramatic effect above. Directions start on Page 124.

The spectacular bed at the right captures the tent-like look so typical of the English Regency period – invoking a style favored since George IV was the fashionable Prince Regent. Chinese motifs were extremely popular, so a Chinoiserie-patterned chintz is very appropriate. Note the dramatic effect of the lining in two contrast-ing colors. Directions for making the scalloped canopy are on Page 127.

DIRECTIONS
FOR WINDOW TREATMENTS

DRAPERIES AND TIEBACKS
ON PAGE 114

MATERIALS NEEDED:
(for each 96"-long pair, to fit 36"-wide window)
- 6½ yards 54"-wide fabric
- 11½ yards 1⅛"-wide, 2-cord shirring tape
- Two ⅜"-diameter brass rings
- Two brass cup hooks
- Large-size drapery hooks
- Adjustable, U-shaped curtain rod

Across full width of fabric, cut two pieces for draperies, each 11" longer than ceiling height, making sure fabric pattern will match. Across full width of fabric, cut two 4"-long pieces for tiebacks.

FOR DRAPERIES:

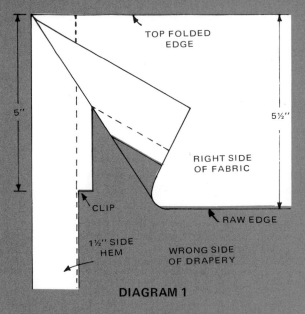

DIAGRAM 1

Turn 2" to wrong side along each selvedge, and clip ½" into selvedge at a point 10½" below top raw edge. Turn selvedge under ½" from clip to bottom edge and stitch 1½" side hem in place, continuing stitching to top raw edge. Turn 5½" at top to wrong side (Diagram 1).

Place strips of shirring tape in positions shown in Diagram 2, folding under raw ends of tape at front edge of drapery. Place bottom row of tape over raw edge of fabric, making sure exposed sections of drawstrings on all three pieces of tape are aligned from top to bottom. Stitch along both edges of each tape, continuing stitching across folded edge at front of drapery to secure drawstrings (see Diagram 2).

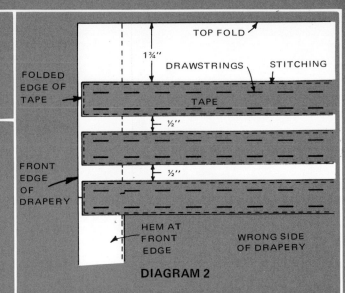

DIAGRAM 2

Turn up a double 3" hem at bottom edge and stitch in place. Make a second panel in same manner, with front edge on opposite side to form a pair. Pull drawstrings to obtain desired width, forming even pleats. Tie drawstrings in a bow and pin out of sight; draperies can be stretched out flat for laundering or dry cleaning. Attach drapery hooks along top row of tape, placing one hook at each end and others about 2" apart.

Attach curtain rod to window frame so top of rod is at proper height to hold top edges of draperies against ceiling when hooks are on rod. Place hooks over rod to hang draperies.

FOR TIEBACKS:
Turn selvedges to wrong sides at short ends of 4" strips, then fold strips to 2" width with raw edges meeting at center; press. Center shirring tape along lengths of tiebacks and stitch in place. Knot drawstrings at one end and pull them up at other end; tie to secure and pin out of sight. Sew a brass ring to center of each end. Attach a cup hook to wall at each side of window at desired height and place rings of tiebacks in hooks.

SWAG AND CASCADE DRAPERY ON PAGE 115

MATERIALS NEEDED:
(for two pair, 36" windows)
- 13 yards 48" fabric
- 13 yards 48" lining fabric
- Staple gun and staples
- Four weights

Cut fabric according to Cutting Diagram. Cut two 38" lengths by full width of fabric to use for swags. Cut four pieces for side cascades to shape and size shown in Diagram 1; cut two as shown, then reverse pattern for other two (see Cutting Diagram). Cut lining fabric to same sizes, two pieces for swags and four for cascades. Cut two pieces of fabric 3" x 43", four pieces 3" x 12" and four pieces 4" x 18" (see Cutting Diagram). Cut pieces of lining fabric to same sizes.

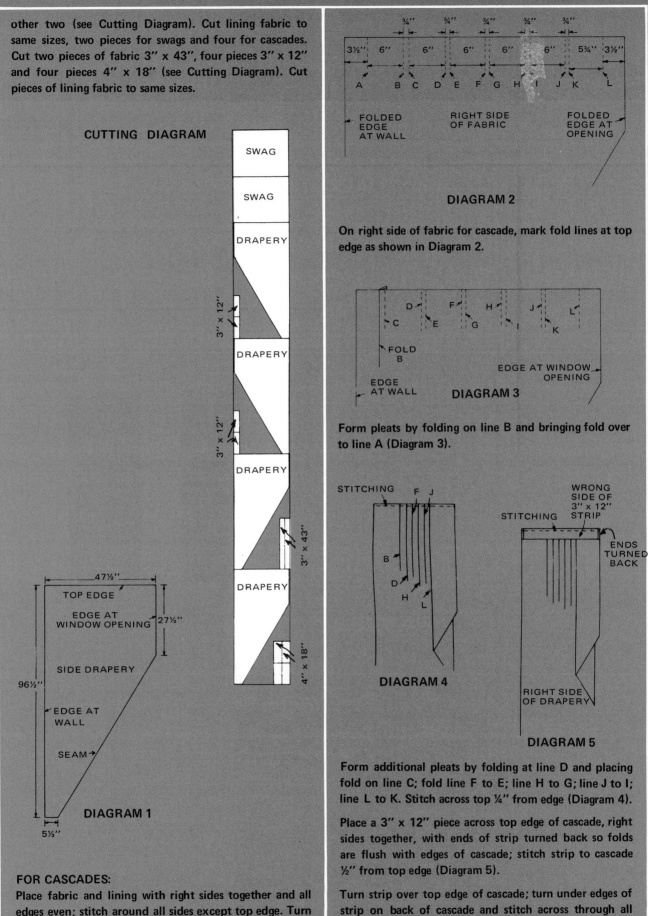

CUTTING DIAGRAM

DIAGRAM 2

On right side of fabric for cascade, mark fold lines at top edge as shown in Diagram 2.

DIAGRAM 3

Form pleats by folding on line B and bringing fold over to line A (Diagram 3).

DIAGRAM 4

DIAGRAM 5

Form additional pleats by folding at line D and placing fold on line C; fold line F to E; line H to G; line J to I; line L to K. Stitch across top ¼" from edge (Diagram 4).

Place a 3" x 12" piece across top edge of cascade, right sides together, with ends of strip turned back so folds are flush with edges of cascade; stitch strip to cascade ½" from top edge (Diagram 5).

Turn strip over top edge of cascade; turn under edges of strip on back of cascade and stitch across through all thicknesses. Make cascade for right side in same manner, reversing markings and directions of pleats across top edge.

DIAGRAM 1

FOR CASCADES:
Place fabric and lining with right sides together and all edges even; stitch around all sides except top edge. Turn right side out and press so seam is along folded edge (see Diagram 1). The following directions are for one cascade for left sides of windows.

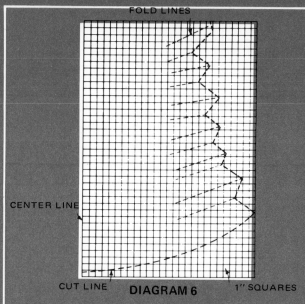

DIAGRAM 6

FOR SWAGS:

Make a paper pattern for one-half of swag, drawing 1"
squares on paper and enlarging pattern from Diagram 6.
(Draw fold lines on pattern.)

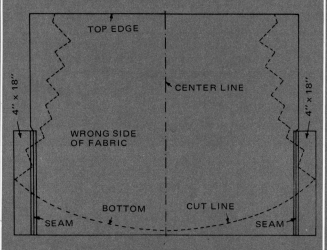

DIAGRAM 7

Stitch 4" x 18" pieces of fabric to lower side edges of
large pieces, taking ½" seams and matching fabric design;
press seams open. Using paper pattern, cut swag
(Diagram 7).

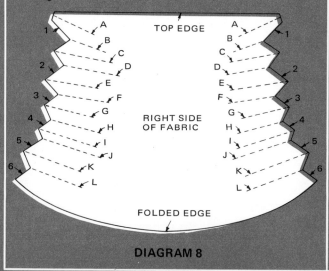

DIAGRAM 8

Seam 4" x 18" pieces of lining fabric to lining in same
manner; cut lining to same pattern as swag. Place fabric
and lining with right sides together and all edges even;
stitch across curved edge at bottom, ½" in from edge.
Turn right side out and press so seam is along folded
edge. Smooth fabric and lining so all edges are even;
baste around all sides. Mark fold lines A through L on
right side of fabric (Diagram 8).

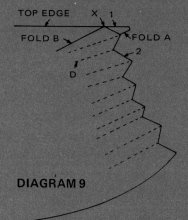

DIAGRAM 9

Fold down on line A and up on line B; bring edge 1 up
so it is even with top edge (Diagram 9). Baste folds and
edges in place at each step (basting is not shown in diagrams to avoid confusion). Point where fold B meets top
edge is point X.

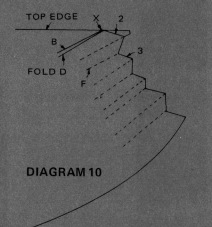

DIAGRAM 10

Fold down along line C and up along line D; bring folded
edge of D to ¼" from X so edge 2 goes to fold line of A
(Diagram 10).

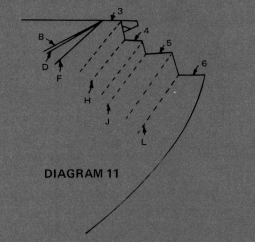

DIAGRAM 11

Fold down on line E and up on line F; bring fold F to ½" from X with edge 3 across top edge (Diagram 11).

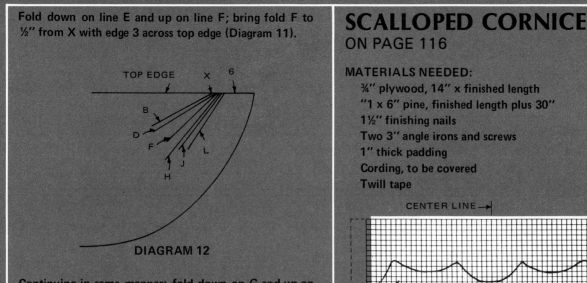

DIAGRAM 12

Continuing in same manner: fold down on G and up on H; bring to ¾" from X with edge 4 along top; fold down on I and up on J; bring J to 1" from X with edge 5 along top; fold down on K and up on L; bring L to top so bottom edge of swag covers end of fold A; piece should measure 20¾" from center to end. Stitch pleats across ¼" from top edge (Diagram 12).

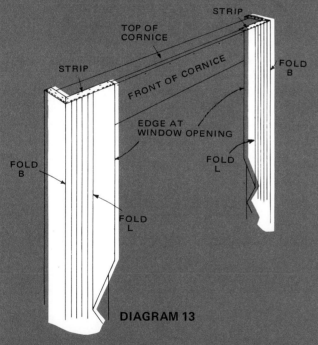

DIAGRAM 13

Pleat other side of swag in same manner. Apply a 3" x 43" piece to top edge of swag in same manner as 3" x 12" piece was applied to side draperies.

Place side cascades on cornice with folded edge B along side front corner, having folded edge at back of cornice go along wall and folded edge at window opening on front of cornice. Place strip at top of cascade on top of cornice and staple in place (Diagram 13).

Place swag across top edge of cornice with strip on top. Staple in place. Attach rod for casement curtains to window frame at required height. Position cornice on angle irons at window and attach with ⅝" screws through angle irons into inside faces of cornice.

SCALLOPED CORNICE
ON PAGE 116

MATERIALS NEEDED:
  ¾" plywood, 14" x finished length
  "1 x 6" pine, finished length plus 30"
  1½" finishing nails
  Two 3" angle irons and screws
  1" thick padding
  Cording, to be covered
  Twill tape

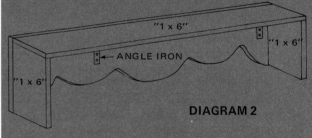

DIAGRAM 1

Cut length of plywood so inside dimension of finished cornice is 4" wider than window frame. Mark 1" squares on plywood and draw scalloped edge of cornice by enlarging squares in Diagram 1. Pattern is for cornice 48" long but can be adapted to longer length by adding up to 3" on each end or by widening scallops (Diagram 1).

DIAGRAM 2

Cut top and two sides from "1 x 6" and assemble cornice as shown in Diagram 2, using 1½" nails. Screw angle irons to underside of top along back edge, about 8" in from each end.

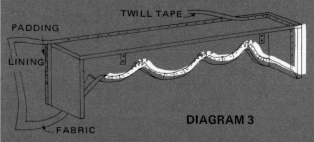

DIAGRAM 3

Place padding on front and trim to shape. Cover with lining and drapery fabric, being careful to center pattern of drapery fabric. Tack fabric to top, then to inside surface of front, starting at widest point and easing fabric around curved scallops and clipping at inside curves. Then pull fabric around ends and tack to inside surfaces. Tack twill tape over raw edge of fabric on top (Diag. 3).

Cut bias strips of fabric and cover cording. Tack cording around bottom edge, then cover raw edges of fabric on inside surfaces with twill tape. Apply fringe to front of cornice, if desired, by blind-stitching it in place. Screw angle irons to window frame in desired position.

PRINT-LINED DRAPERIES
ON PAGE 117

MATERIALS NEEDED:
- Poles and brackets
- Rings and hooks
- Weights
- Two ⅜" brass rings
- Two brass cup hooks

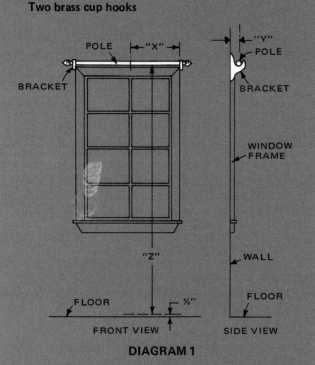

DIAGRAM 1

Attach rod across top of window in desired position. Measure distance from center of window to inside of bracket for dimension "X". Measure from wall to center of pole for return "Y". Measure from bottom of pole to ½" from floor for length "Z" (Diagram 1).

Cut lengths of plain fabric 7" longer than Z. Seam together to obtain width equal to three times X plus Y plus 2". Cut and seam printed fabric together to same size, matching pattern carefully.

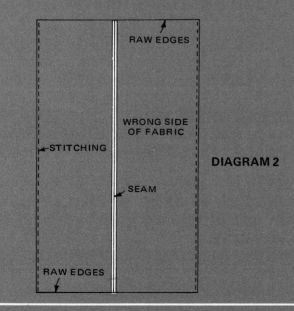

DIAGRAM 2

Place printed and plain fabrics with right sides together and stitch down each side, ½" from edge (Diagram 2). Press seams open.

Stitch across top, ½" from edge. Turn draperies right side out and press so seams are along edges. Divide measurement "X" from Diagram 1 into equal parts (3½" to 4" each) to determine width of A sections.

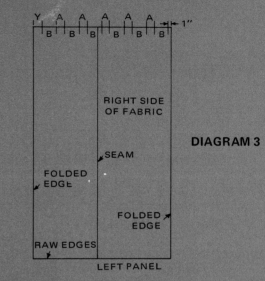

DIAGRAM 3

Double measurement X and divide into equal parts to determine width of B sections so there is one more B section than A. For example: If section "X" has five 4" A sections, divide twice "X" by 6 to determine size of B sections. To mark off pleats, start at right edge of left panel. Measure 1", then B and A alternately across, ending with Y at left edge (Diagram 3).

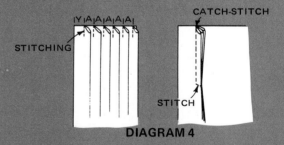

DIAGRAM 4

Fold B sections in half, bringing A lines together and stitch 4" down from top edge. Fold fullness of pleat into three equal smaller folds. Stitch across lower edge of folds and catch-stitch inside of folds at top (Diagram 4).

Make remainder of pleats. Make right panel in same manner, marking from left edge of panel, with Y at right side. Place rings on pole and attach hooks to draperies at each pleat.

BED DRAPERY AND BEDSPREAD ON PAGE 118

MATERIALS NEEDED:
- 3 pieces "1 x 3" pine x width of bed plus 20" for A, B, and C
- Nine toggle bolts

Snap tape and ½" cording
Zipper for bolster
Finishing nails
Four ½" brass rings
Two curtain rods
Flannel interfacing
Lining fabric (sateen, muslin or polished cotton)

PLEATED PANEL BEHIND BED:

Nail A to B with finishing nails as shown in Diagram 1. Tack snap tape around three edges of A and across B, having snaps as close to ends as possible and placing tape on B as close to corner as you can (Diagram 2). Attach A and B to wall and ceiling with three toggle bolts through each piece. Attach lower strip C to wall with toggle bolts in the same manner, so it is located 3" below the top edge of mattress (Diagram 3).

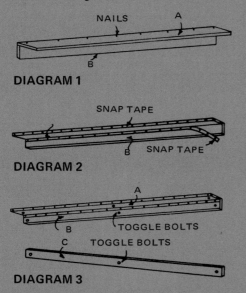

Cut fabric lengths to height required (top of A to bottom of C) plus 2" and seam pieces together to make one piece three times width of B plus 2". Make 1" hem down each side and press seams open. Make 2" deep pleats across top and bottom edges, keeping seams on the inside of pleats. Stitch snap tape across top and bottom edges on right side, having inside edge of tape 1" in from edge of fabric (Diagram 4).

Tack snap tape along bottom edge of C, then snap tapes on the pleated panel to tapes tacked to B and C (Diagram 5).

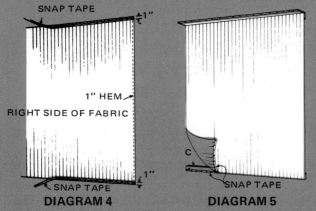

PLEATED DUST RUFFLE

Measure top of bed (over sheets and blankets) from head to foot and from side to side. Cut fabric to fit top of bed, plus ⅝" on all four sides, seaming fabric down the center if necessary. Press seam open and make a ⅝" hem across one short edge for head of bed. Measure from top of bed to floor and add 3" for hem (seam allowance along top edge will raise ruffle enough to clear floor). Cutting across width of fabric, cut pieces to this measurement and seam them together until piece is long enough to go around three sides of the bed after 2" deep pleats have been made. Press seams open, make 1" hem down both side edges and a 3" hem along bottom edge. With right sides together, sew pleated edge of ruffle to top, making a ⅝" seam (Diagram 6).

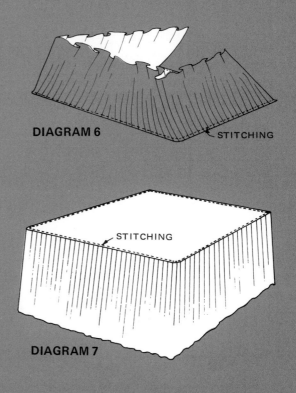

Turn ruffle right side out and stitch around three sides ½" in from seam line, making sure seam allowances and pleats are stitched flat to the wrong side of top section (Diagram 7).

COVERLET:

Measure top of bed as before, having ruffle in place. Cut fabric, flannel interfacing and lining fabric to fit top of bed plus seam allowances, seaming if necessary and matching pattern on outer fabric carefully. Cut strips of outer fabric one-half the depth of ruffle and seam together until long enough to go around three sides of the bed. Cut interfacing and lining fabric the same size. Press all seams open.

Draw scalloped design on outer fabric so a scallop goes around each corner at the foot and one is in the center. Continue scallop design along both sides.

Cut bias strips and cover cording. Place cording along scalloped edge and stitch, clipping seam allowance of

cording as needed to go around curves. Trim fabric ⅝"
outside of stitching line (Diagram 8).

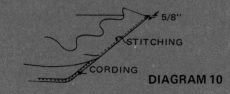

DIAGRAM 8

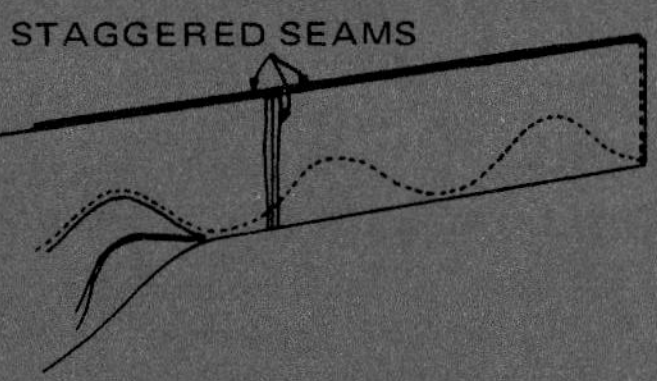

DIAGRAM 9

Place lining fabric wrong side down on interfacing; then
place outer fabric right side down on lining. Be sure to
stagger seams so they do not fall on top of each other,
then baste all three pieces together. Stitch ⅝" seam
down each side, then stitch along scalloped edge following stitched line where cording was applied. Trim away
extra lining fabric and interfacing (Diagram 9). Clip inner curved edges and turn right side out, then press.

DIAGRAM 10

Baste interfacing to wrong side of top piece. Stitch cording to three edges, taking a ⅝" seam and clipping seam
allowance of cording to go around corners. Stitch scalloped drop to top along same stitching line (Diagram
10), keeping ends of drop ⅝" in from head end of top
piece.

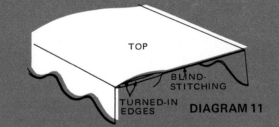

DIAGRAM 11

Fold scalloped drop back over top, then baste lining
fabric (right side down) along three edges of top, enclos-
ing drop. Turn right side out to make certain top lies
smooth and flat. When lining is properly basted to top,
stitch around three sides on same stitching line as before.
Turn right side out and press. Turn under edges across
head of bed and blind-stitch (Diagram 11).

BED DRAPERY:
Cut fabric to desired width plus 4" for side hem and to
desired length plus 3" for hem. Cut lining 3" shorter
than outer fabric and 8" narrower. Turn up 3" hem in
outer fabric and a 1" hem in lining. Matching side and
top edges, right sides together, seam from top to bottom
of lining hem (Diagram 12). Press seams open and fold
so seams are same distance from side folds on both sides.
Stitch ⅝" seam across top (Diagram 13). Turn right side
out and press. Make pleats across top edge.

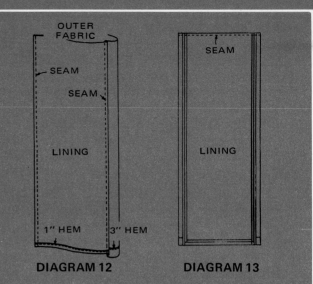

DIAGRAM 12   **DIAGRAM 13**

Cut tie-backs as shown in Diagram 14, making two of
outer fabric and two of lining fabric. Stitch cording to
right side of outer fabric, ⅝" from edge, across top and
bottom edges.

Place lining fabric on outer fabric, right sides together,
and stitch along same stitching line. Turn right side out.
Turn in ends and blind-stitch closed. Sew brass ring on
each end (Diagram 15).

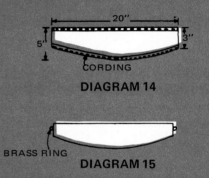

DIAGRAM 14

DIAGRAM 15

Attach curtain rod to each end of B and hang draperies.
Screw cup hook to wall at each side of bed and hook
rings of tie-back over them.

VALANCE:
Cut strips of fabric, interfacing and lining to same depth
as scalloped drop for spread and long enough to go
around three sides of A plus seam allowances. Space
scallops so lowest points are at equal thirds of width. Assemble in same manner as for scalloped drop of spread.

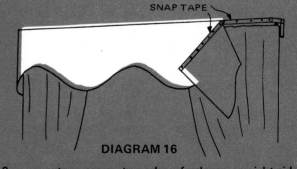

DIAGRAM 16

Sew snap tape across top edge of valance on right side
so snaps match those on tape attached to A. Turn taped
edge under and snap valance in place on A (Diagram 16).

SCALLOPED BED CANOPY

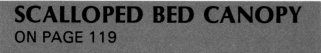

MATERIALS NEEDED:
- Two "1 x 3" pine x length of bed
- Two "1 x 3" pine x width of bed
- One "1 x 3" pine x width of bed less 1½"
- Twelve 1½" flat head screws
- Six toggle bolts
- Six 1½" angle irons and screws
- Upholsterer's tape
- Curtain rods

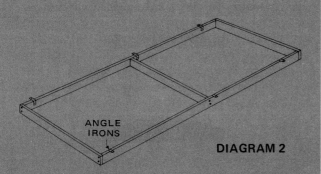

SCREWS

DIAGRAM 1

Assemble "1 x 3" frame as shown in Diagram 1 by attaching the ends to the sides with two screws at each corner. Attach center support with two screws at each end. Countersink screw heads.

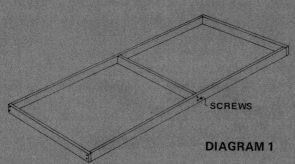

ANGLE IRONS

DIAGRAM 2

Attach angle irons to inside of frame as shown in Diagram 2, placing two on each side about 6" from ends and one on each side close to center support.

DIAGRAM 3

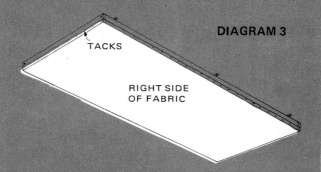

TACKS

RIGHT SIDE OF FABRIC

Cut solid-color fabric to size of frame plus 2" on all sides; seam fabric if necessary and press seam open. Cover under side of frame with fabric, wrong side against frame, by stretching it across frame and up onto sides and ends. Staple or tack fabric in place along raw edge, mitering corners (Diagram 3).

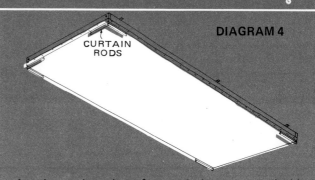

DIAGRAM 4

CURTAIN RODS

Attach curtain rods to frame, placing one at each side next to head of frame which will be against wall, and two at each corner of other end (Diagram 4). Attach frame to ceiling with toggle bolts through the angle irons. Paint ends of angle irons to match ceiling.

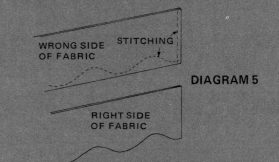

WRONG SIDE OF FABRIC   **STITCHING**

DIAGRAM 5

RIGHT SIDE OF FABRIC

To make scalloped valance, cut drapery fabric and lining long enough to go around three sides of frame plus 1¼" by depth of scallops plus 1⅝". Place right sides of fabric and lining together and draw desired scallop design, with lowest point of scallops ⅝" from bottom edge of fabric, spacing scallops so they will be centered on both sides and end of canopy (see photograph on Page 119). Stitch from top of valance down to scalloped edge on both ends, taking ⅝" seams. Stitch along outline of scallops. Turn valance right side out and press (Diag. 5).

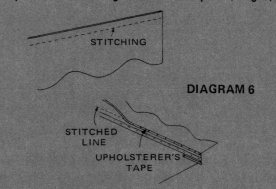

STITCHING

DIAGRAM 6

STITCHED LINE

UPHOLSTERER'S TAPE

Stitch across top of valance through both fabrics 1" from raw edges. With right side of valance against ceiling, place stitched line along top edge of frame, then tack upholsterer's tape to frame through 1" allowance, with top edge of tape along same stitched line (Diagram 6). Applying upholsterer's tape along top edge of frame will insure a straight, even line along top of valance when you let it hang down to cover frame.

Make lined draperies for each corner of canopy and hang on insides of curtain rods so rods are concealed from inside. Make tie-backs and attach to draperies.